PABLO NERUDA

I Explain a Few Things

Selected Poems

PABLO NERUDA (1904–1973) was born in Parral, central Chile. His father was a railway worker and his mother, who died when Neruda was a child, was a schoolteacher. He was educated at the Instituto Pedagógico in Santiago and at the University of Chile. Neruda is among the most widely translated poets in the world. His celebrated collections include *Twenty Love Poems and a Song of Despair*, *Residence on Earth*, *Canto General*, *Elemental Odes*, *One Hundred Love Sonnets*, and *Fully Empowered*; he is also the author of two nonfiction works, *Memoirs* and *Passions and Impressions*. Neruda was the recipient of many honors during his lifetime, including the World Peace Prize, with Paul Robeson and Pablo Picasso, in 1950. He was awarded the Nobel Prize in Literature in 1971. He died in 1973, age sixty-nine, in Santiago.

ILAN STAVANS is the Lewis-Sebring Professor in Latin American and Latino Culture and Five College–40th Anniversary Professor at Amherst College. His books include *The Hispanic Condition* (1995), *The Riddle of Cantinflas* (1998), *On Borrowed Words* (2001), *Spanglish* (2003), *Dictionary Days* (2005), and *The Disappearance* (2006). He edited the three-volume *Isaac Bashevis Singer: Collected Stories*, as well as the four-volume *Encyclopedia Latina*. His work has been translated into a dozen languages. Routledge published *The Essential Ilan Stavans* in 2000. He received Chile's Presidential Medal for *The Poetry of Pablo Neruda* (FSG, 2003).

I Explain a Few Things

Translators

ROBERT BLY

JOHN FELSTINER

GALWAY KINNELL

PHILIP LEVINE

W. S. MERWIN

WILLIAM O'DALY

MARGARET SAYERS PEDEN

ALASTAIR REID

JACK SCHMITT

ILAN STAVANS

STEPHEN TAPSCOTT

DONALD D. WALSH

I Explain
a Few Things

PABLO NERUDA

Selected Poems

EDITED BY ILAN STAVANS

FARRAR, STRAUS AND GIROUX

New York

FARRAR, STRAUS AND GIROUX
19 Union Square West, New York 10003

This work contains poems from the following original volumes by Pablo
Neruda: *Veinte poemas de amor y una canción desesperada* (1924),
Residencia en la tierra (1933), *Tercera residencia* (1947), *Canto general*
(1950), *Los versos del capitán* (1952), *Odas elementales* (1954), *Nuevas odas
elementales* (1956), *Tercer libro de odas* (1957), *Estravagario* (1958),
Navegaciones y regresos (1959), *Cien sonetos de amor* (1959), *Plenos
poderes* (1962), *Memorial de Isla Negra* (1964), *Arte de pájaros* (1966), *Las
manos del día* (1968), *Fin del mundo* (1969), *Jardín de invierno* (1974),
Defectos escogidos (1974).

Owing to limitations of space, all acknowledgments for permission to
reprint previously published material can be found on pages 353–355.

Library of Congress Cataloging-in-Publication Data
Neruda, Pablo, 1904–1973.
[Poems. English & Spanish. Selections]
I explain a few things : selected poems / Pablo Neruda ; edited by Ilan
Stavans. — 1st ed.
p. cm.
Includes index.
ISBN-13: 978-0-374-26079-8 (pbk. : alk. paper)
ISBN-10: 0-374-26079-6 (pbk. : alk. paper)
1. Neruda, Pablo, 1904–1973—Translations into English. I. Stavans,
Ilan. II. Title.

PQ8097 .N4A2 2007
816' .64—dc22

2006039101

Designed by Gretchen Achilles

www.fsgbooks.com

1   3   5   7   9   10   8   6   4   2

Contents

vii

FROM

Estravagario / Extravagaria
(1957-58)

FROM

Navegaciones y regresos / Navigations and Returns
(1957-59)

FROM

Cien sonetos de amor / One Hundred Love Sonnets
(1957-59)

FROM

Plenos poderes / Fully Empowered
(1961–62)

Preface

"LADIES AND GENTLEMEN, I never found in books any formula for writing poetry; and I, in turn, do not intend to leave in print a word of advice, a method, or a style that will allow young poets to receive from me some drop of supposed wisdom." Thus spoke Pablo Neruda on December 13, 1971, upon receiving the Nobel Prize for Literature. He had become by then the Latin American poet par excellence, a Walt Whitman of the Spanish language. The Stockholm committee acknowledged Neruda "for a poetry that with the action of an elemental force brings alive a continent's destiny and dreams." That continent was known—maybe still is—for being trapped in a hundred-year labyrinth of solitude. But Neruda added: "There is no unassailable solitude. All roads lead to the same point: to the communication of who we are. And we must travel across lonely and rugged terrain, through isolation and silence, to reach the magic zone where we can dance an awkward dance."

It was clear at Neruda's centennial, celebrated in 2004, that his journey has never been more tangible. He is the emblem of the engaged poet, an artist whose heart, always with the people, is consumed by passion. That passion is defined by politics. Gabriel García Márquez called him "the best poet of the twentieth century—in any language." The blurb might be overinflated. There is already little doubt, though, that Neruda is among the most lasting voices of that most tumultuous (in his own words, "the saddest") century. He is surely one of the most popular poets of all time; his books, from his romantic *Twenty Love Poems and a Song of Despair* to his masterpiece *The Heights of Macchu Picchu*, and his memorable and endlessly mutating poems about Isla Negra sell millions of copies in dozens of countries.

Even before his death in 1973, at the age of sixty-nine, Neruda was an icon of the young: at once eternally idealistic and impossibly hyperkinetic. Among his own idols was Walt Whitman, whom he called an "essential brother." Whitman personified for Neruda the crossroads where poetry and politics meet—or don't—and the commitment to use the pen as a calibrator of one's age. After a self-centered start, he published *Canto general*, the endeavor that made him dutifully famous, written over a decade (1938–49) that spanned the atrocities and war crimes of World War II. *Canto general* offered a CinemaScope portrait of the Americas, the United States included, that still is unprecedented. Everything is included: its mineral structure, its flora and fauna, the tribal struggles of its pre-Columbian past, the sweeping swords of the conquistadors and liberators, and a picture of average workers in factories at midcentury, anonymous in their jobs or on strikes to improve their miserable labor conditions. Though Borges and Neruda are polar opposites, there is something almost Borgesian in Neruda's task: yes, as the Nobel announcement had it, he attempted to reduce the universe—or at least *a* universe—into a single book. Poetry today appears to have lost that ambition, supplanting it with an endless need to emphasize the autobiographical. Creative writing workshops do little but manufacture inane poems by consent. In spite of his refusal to leave us a manual of style, Neruda's oeuvre displays a clear pedagogy: it puts poetry and history side by side.

This isn't to say that Neruda is foolproof. The evidence points to the contrary. His best poems feel as if created by one who is not as temperate as one is likely to imagine. He also left us an overdose of bad poetry. How could he not when his five-volume *Obras completas*, published in Spanish in 1999, totals some six thousand pages? While editing *The Poetry of Pablo Neruda*, published in 2003, I often thought of Truman Capote's comment on Jack Kerouac: he didn't write, Capote said, he simply typed. Neruda's late oeuvre is passable at best and disheveled at worst. Indeed Alastair Reid, one of Neruda's most accomplished English translators, told me I was doing a disservice by releasing, in between covers, an excess of six hundred poems by the Chilean laureate, organized so as to show the overall arc of his career. However, an unsmoothed Neruda is better than a censored Neruda, even when that censorship has nothing to do with politics and all to do with aesthetics. To fully appreciate the sublime, it helps to meddle with the unworthy.

The most attractive yet delicate aspect of Neruda's posterity has to do with his ideological odyssey. He was simultaneously a witness and a chronicler of most of the decisive events of the twentieth century. From the remoteness of his childhood he heard the bangs of the Great War, was a published poet in Spain in the 1930s (he befriended Federico García Lorca), traveled through the Soviet Union, saw the rise and demise of Hitler, made it to Cuba after 1959, opposed the U.S. invasion of Vietnam and Cambodia, and was in Chile when General Augusto Pinochet orchestrated a coup—on the other 9/11—against the elected Socialist president Salvador Allende. In fact, Neruda often posed as a politician: he was a senator in Chile and also a presidential hopeful; and at various moments and different geographies he was a diplomat.

None of which managed to dissipate his naïveté. In a poem he imagines Franco in hell: "May you be alone and accursed, /

alone and awake among all the dead, / and let blood fall upon you like rain, / and let a dying river of severed eyes / slide and flow over you staring at you endlessly." He was a staunch supporter of Stalin, which prompted him to write cheap red propaganda. He imprudently embraces Fidel Castro: "Fidel, Fidel, the people are grateful / for word in action and deeds that sing, / that is why I bring from far / a cup of my country's wine." And in the early 1970s he wrote a book called, embarrassingly, *Incitación al Nixonicidio*—in English, "Invitation to the Nixonicide."

Still, Neruda is a torch-bearer. On campus in the 1970s he was a favorite. The beatniks made him a role model. But then the neoliberals of the 1980s turned him into an archaism. In 1995 came Michael Radford's film *Il Postino*, based on a novella by Neruda's compatriot Antonio Skármeta. Since then he has enjoyed a renewed appeal, intensified by the festivities surrounding his centennial. Students embrace him because he sought fairness and didn't shy away from resistance. The Communism that Neruda so fervently championed has lost its gravitas, but another larger-than-life conflict has taken hold. How would he react to the current atmosphere where civil liberties are under threat in our country, which prides itself on being fundamentally democratic? And what would his take be on the misconstrued War on Terror? In his Nobel speech he said he had no manual to offer to the next generation. His poetry is anything but programmatic: it is fluid, rambunctious, centrifugal.

His unstoppable commitment to freedom during the Spanish Civil War has enormous currency nowadays. After the terrorist bombings in Madrid in March 2004, the electorate voted José María Aznar out of office in a clear rebuttal of his foreign policy in Iraq. Neruda's indictment of careless corporate globalism in poems like "United Fruit Co." has, if anything, become more urgent. And his anger against limitations on press freedom, from

Venezuela to Saudi Arabia, North Korea and the United States, feels as if it had been expressed just this morning. I'm especially drawn to Neruda's deep if conflicted love toward *el coloso del norte*, the English-speaking America. Throughout his life he made sure to distinguish between the people of the United States and its government. He honored the honesty and noblesse in the American masses but reacted irritably when that honesty and noblesse were betrayed by politicos. In "I Wish the Woodcutter Would Wake Up," Neruda states, "What we love is your peace, not your mask." He stresses the element of peace again, putting it—in Robert Bly's translation—in a larger context:

> *You come, like a washerwoman, from*
> *a simple cradle, near your rivers, pale.*
> *Built up from the unknown,*
> *what is sweet in you is your hivelike peace.*
> *We love the man with his hands red*
> *from the Oregon clay, your Negro boy*
> *who brought you the music born*
> *in his country of tusks: we love*
> *your city, your substance,*
> *your light, your machines, the energy . . .*

Then, of course, there's the domestic Neruda, whose "elemental odes" are, well, elemental; they celebrate with Buddhist concentration the mundane, insignificant objects surrounding us: a stamp album, an artichoke, a hare-boy, a watermelon, a bee, a village movie theater . . . What do they say about us? And what do we, their enablers, say about them? I presume it's my trade, but the ones I never stop rereading are the odes to the book ("A book ripens and falls / like all fruits, / it has light / and shadow"), the ode to the dictionary ("you are not a / tomb, sepulcher, grave, / tumulus, mausoleum, / but guard and keeper, / hidden fire"), and the two odes to criticism ("With a single life / I will not learn enough. / With the light of other lives, / many lives will live in my song"). These are items always at our side, yet somehow Neruda makes us see them anew.

Over time, I've learned to understand an aspect in Neruda that I had failed to spot and that my students recurrently point to: his humor. This aspect on occasion appears connected to religion, which, needless to say, was not his dish *du jour*, a factor that highlights one of Neruda's limitations in reaching readers today. He ignored God and dismissed faith as irrelevant. After reading dozens of his poems compressed into a single semester, a student of mine said, a bit pompously, "A life experienced only through the heart is nothing but tragedy; one approached solely through the mind is comedy; and one seen through Neruda's eyes is sheer drama—poignant and droll." What mesmerized the student was that the Chilean bard had resisted, to the extent that is possible, the traps of cynicism. He took human behavior seriously and knew how to laugh.

As death approached him, perhaps he did become sarcastic. In "The Great Urinator," a poem he wrote while suffering from prostate cancer and that he left unpublished (it is part of the posthumous *Selected Failings*), he portrays God peeing bronze-colored, dense liquid rain from above. The urine falls on factories, cemeteries, and gardens, as well as churches. It flows inexhaustibly underneath doors and in avenues, backing up drains, disintegrating marble floors, carpets, and staircases. It is a scene taken out of a Hollywood disaster movie: How do people react? Neruda's answer is hilarious: Everyone is frightened, but oops, there are no umbrellas. And "from on high the great urinator," the poem states (in John Felstiner's rendition), "was silent." What does all this mean? True to form, Neruda doesn't sort out the imbroglio. Again, he has no wisdom to dispense. Or has he? The last stanzas read:

I am a pale and artless poet
not here to work out riddles
or recommend special umbrellas.

Hasta la vista! I greet you and go off
to a country where they won't ask me questions.

The more than fifty poems I've collected in this bilingual anthology are representative of Neruda's diverse, multitudinous career, ranging from the intimate to the denunciatory. My objective has been to distill the poet's exuberance to its most essential while producing a book affordable to young people. At almost one thousand pages and with a tag of $40 on its hardcover edition, *The Poetry of Pablo Neruda* was my source. Still, I've departed from it in that *I Explain a Few Things* includes some new translations, as well as a handful of previously unavailable poems in English such as "Ode to the Eye." The translator's name appears at the end of each English version. The material is organized chronologically by the poem's original book source: "I Ask for Silence," for instance, appears as part of *Extravagaria*. The years listed in parentheses in the table of contents refer not to dated publication but to the period in which Neruda wrote a particular book.

The title comes from a defining poem in Neruda's book *Third Residence*, usually incorporated into the more ambitious *Residence on Earth*. A benchmark in the Chilean's oeuvre, it is a manifesto renouncing the romantic tonalities of *Twenty Love Poems and a Song of Despair* and an embrace of the type of ideological poetry with which he would be identified for the rest of his life. In it Neruda is at his most domestic—it has a house as its leitmotif—while also striving to confront the impact of the Spanish Civil War on him and his entire generation. The personal and the universal are juxtaposed in just the exact way. It is, undoubtedly, one of my own favorite poems. The title also encompasses Neruda's humble approach to art, making it heartfelt and confessional, a journey of self-discovery. Plus, it articulates his moral dilemma in appropriate fashion: how does one make art out of tragedy?

—I.S.

Veinte poemas de amor y una canción desesperada

Twenty Love Poems and a Song of Despair

(1923-24)

XV ME GUSTAS CUANDO CALLAS

Me gustas cuando callas porque estás como ausente,
y me oyes desde lejos, y mi voz no te toca.
Parece que los ojos se te hubieran volado
y parece que un beso te cerrara la boca.

Como todas las cosas están llenas de mi alma
emerges de las cosas, llena del alma mía.
Mariposa de sueño, te pareces a mi alma,
y te pareces a la palabra melancolía.

Me gustas cuando callas y estás como distante.
Y estás como quejándote, mariposa en arrullo.
Y me oyes desde lejos, y mi voz no te alcanza:
déjame que me calle con el silencio tuyo.

Déjame que te hable también con tu silencio
claro como una lámpara, simple como un anillo.
Eres como la noche, callada y constelada.
Tu silencio es de estrella, tan lejano y sencillo.

Me gustas cuando callas porque estás como ausente.
Distante y dolorosa como si hubieras muerto.
Una palabra entonces, una sonrisa bastan.
Y estoy alegre, alegre de que no sea cierto.

XV I LIKE FOR YOU TO BE STILL

I like for you to be still: it is as though you were absent,
and you hear me from far away and my voice does not touch you.
It seems as though your eyes had flown away
and it seems that a kiss had sealed your mouth.

As all things are filled with my soul
you emerge from the things, filled with my soul.
You are like my soul, a butterfly of dream,
and you are like the word Melancholy.

I like for you to be still, and you seem far away.
It sounds as though you were lamenting, a butterfly cooing like a
    dove.
And you hear me from far away, and my voice does not reach you:
Let me come to be still in your silence.

And let me talk to you with your silence
that is bright as a lamp, simple as a ring.
You are like the night, with its stillness and constellations.
Your silence is that of a star, as remote and candid.

I like for you to be still: it is as though you were absent,
distant and full of sorrow as though you had died.
One word then, one smile, is enough.
And I am happy, happy that it's not true.

W. S. MERWIN

XX PUEDO ESCRIBIR

Puedo escribir los versos más tristes esta noche.

Escribir, por ejemplo: «La noche está estrellada,
y tiritan, azules, los astros, a lo lejos».

El viento de la noche gira en el cielo y canta.

Puedo escribir los versos más tristes esta noche.
Yo la quise, y a veces ella también me quiso.

En las noches como ésta la tuve entre mis brazos.
La besé tantas veces bajo el cielo infinito.

Ella me quiso, a veces yo también la quería.
Cómo no haber amado sus grandes ojos fijos.

Puedo escribir los versos más tristes esta noche.
Pensar que no la tengo. Sentir que la he perdido.

Oír la noche inmensa, más inmensa sin ella.
Y el verso cae al alma como al pasto el rocío.

Qué importa que mi amor no pudiera guardarla.
La noche está estrellada y ella no está conmigo.

Eso es todo. A lo lejos alguien canta. A lo lejos.
Mi alma no se contenta con haberla perdido.

XX TONIGHT I CAN WRITE

repetition
senses = soul
metaphors

Tonight I can write the saddest lines.

Write, for example, "The night is starry
and the stars are blue and shiver in the distance."

The night wind revolves in the sky and sings.

Tonight I can write the saddest lines.
I loved her, and sometimes she loved me too.

inner and external thoughts of one person.

Through nights like this one I held her in my arms.
I kissed her again and again under the endless sky.

She loved me, sometimes I loved her too.
How could one not have loved her great still eyes.

Tonight I can write the saddest lines.
To think that I do not have her. To feel that I have lost her.

To hear the immense night, still more immense without her.
And the verse falls to the soul like dew to the pasture.

What does it matter that my love could not keep her.
The night is starry and she is not with me.

This is all. In the distance someone is singing. In the distance.
My soul is not satisfied that it has lost her.

Como para acercarla mi mirada la busca.
Mi corazón la busca, y ella no está conmigo.

La misma noche que hace blanquear los mismos árboles.
Nosotros, los de entonces, ya no somos los mismos.

Ya no la quiero, es cierto, pero cuánto la quise.
Mi voz buscaba el viento para tocar su oído.

De otro. Será de otro. Como antes de mis besos.
Su voz, su cuerpo claro. Sus ojos infinitos.

Ya no la quiero, es cierto, pero tal vez la quiero.
Es tan corto el amor, y es tan largo el olvido.

Porque en noches como ésta la tuve entre mis brazos,
mi alma no se contenta con haberla perdido.

Aunque éste sea el último dolor que ella me causa,
y éstos sean los últimos versos que yo le escribo.

My sight tries to find her as though to bring her closer.
My heart looks for her, and she is not with me.

The same night whitening the same trees.
We, of that time, are no longer the same.

I no longer love her, that's certain, but how I loved her.
My voice tried to find the wind to touch her hearing.

Another's. She will be another's. As she was before my kisses.
Her voice, her bright body. Her infinite eyes.

I no longer love her, that's certain, but maybe I love her.
Love is so short, forgetting is so long.

Because through nights like this one I held her in my arms
my soul is not satisfied that it has lost her.

Though this be the last pain that she makes me suffer
and these the last verses that I write for her.

W. S. MERWIN

7

FROM

Residencia en
la tierra

Residence on
Earth

(1925-35)

ARTE POÉTICA

Entre sombra y espacio, entre guarniciones y doncellas,
dotado de corazón singular y sueños funestos,
precipitadamente pálido, marchito en la frente,
y con luto de viudo furioso por cada día de vida,
ay, para cada agua invisible que bebo soñolientamente,
y de todo sonido que acojo temblando,
tengo la misma sed ausente y la misma fiebre fría,
un oído que nace, una angustia indirecta,
como si llegaran ladrones o fantasmas,
y en una cáscara de extensión fija y profunda,
como un camarero humillado, como una campana un poco ronca,
como un espejo viejo, como un olor de casa sola
en la que los huéspedes entran de noche perdidamente ebrios,
y hay un olor de ropa tirada al suelo, y una ausencia de flores,
posiblemente de otro modo aún menos melancólico,
pero, la verdad, de pronto, el viento que azota mi pecho,
las noches de substancia infinita caídas en mi dormitorio,
el ruido de un día que arde con sacrificio,
me piden lo profético que hay en mí, con melancolía,
y un golpe de objetos que llaman sin ser respondidos
hay, y un movimiento sin tregua, y un nombre confuso.

Between shadow and space, between trimmings and damsels,
endowed with a singular heart and sorrowful dreams,
precipitously pallid, withered in the brow
and with a furious widower's mourning for each day of life,
ah, for each invisible water that I drink somnolently
and from every sound that I welcome trembling,
I have the same absent thirst and the same cold fever,
a nascent ear, an indirect anguish,
as if thieves or ghosts were coming,
and in a shell of fixed and profound expanse,
like a humiliated waiter, like a slightly raucous bell,
like an old mirror, like the smell of a solitary house
where the guests come in at night wildly drunk,
and there is a smell of clothes thrown on the floor, and an absence of
    flowers—
possibly in another even less melancholy way—
but the truth is that suddenly the wind that lashes my chest,
the nights of infinite substance fallen in my bedroom,
the noise of a day that burns with sacrifice,
ask me mournfully what prophecy there is in me,
and there is a swarm of objects that call without being answered,
and a ceaseless movement, and a bewildered man.

DONALD D. WALSH

11

Sucede que me canso de ser hombre.
Sucede que entro en las sastrerías y en los cines
marchito, impenetrable, como un cisne de fieltro
navegando en un agua de origen y ceniza.

El olor de las peluquerías me hace llorar a gritos.
Sólo quiero un descanso de piedras o de lana,
sólo quiero no ver establecimientos ni jardines,
ni mercaderías, ni anteojos, ni ascensores.

Sucede que me canso de mis pies y mis uñas
y mi pelo y mi sombra.
Sucede que me canso de ser hombre.

Sin embargo sería delicioso
asustar a un notario con un lirio cortado
o dar muerte a una monja con un golpe de oreja.
Sería bello
ir por las calles con un cuchillo verde
y dando gritos hasta morir de frío.

No quiero seguir siendo raíz en las tinieblas,
vacilante, extendido, tiritando de sueño,
hacia abajo, en las tripas mojadas de la tierra,
absorbiendo y pensando, comiendo cada día.

No quiero para mí tantas desgracias.
No quiero continuar de raíz y de tumba,

∘ repetitions
∘ what does it mean to be a man?

It so happens I am sick of being a man.
And it happens that I walk into tailorshops and movie houses
dried up, waterproof, like a swan made of felt
steering my way in a water of wombs and ashes.

The smell of barbershops makes me break into hoarse sobs.
The only thing I want is to lie still like stones or wool,
The only thing I want is to see no more stores, no gardens,
no more goods, no spectacles, no elevators.

It so happens I am sick of my feet and my nails
and my hair and my shadow.
It so happens I am sick of being a man.

Still it would be marvelous
to terrify a law clerk with a cut lily,
or kill a nun with a blow on the ear.
It would be great
to go through the streets with a green knife
letting out yells until I died of the cold.

∘ different use of similes and metaphors

I don't want to go on being a root in the dark,
insecure, stretched out, shivering with sleep,
going on down, into the moist guts of the earth,
taking in and thinking, eating every day.

I don't want so much misery.
I don't want to go on as a root and a tomb,

13

de subterráneo solo, de bodega con muertos
ateridos, muriéndome de pena.

Por eso el día lunes arde como el petróleo
cuando me ve llegar con mi cara de cárcel,
y aúlla en su transcurso como una rueda herida,
y da pasos de sangre caliente hacia la noche.

Y me empuja a ciertos rincones, a ciertas casas húmedas,
a hospitales donde los huesos salen por la ventana,
a ciertas zapaterías con olor a vinagre,
a calles espantosas como grietas.

Hay pájaros de color de azufre y horribles intestinos
colgando de las puertas de las casas que odio,
hay dentaduras olvidadas en una cafetera,
hay espejos
que debieran haber llorado de vergüenza y espanto,
hay paraguas en todas partes, y venenos, y ombligos.

Yo paseo con calma, con ojos, con zapatos,
con furia, con olvido,
paso, cruzo oficinas y tiendas de ortopedia,
y patios donde hay ropas colgadas de un alambre:
calzoncillos, toallas y camisas que lloran
lentas lágrimas sucias.

alone under the ground, a warehouse with corpses,
half frozen, dying of grief.

That's why Monday, when it sees me coming
with my convict face, blazes up like gasoline,
and it howls on its way like a wounded wheel,
and leaves tracks full of warm blood leading toward the night.

And it pushes me into certain corners, into some moist houses,
into hospitals where the bones fly out the window,
into shoeshops that smell like vinegar,
and certain streets hideous as cracks in the skin.

There are sulfur-colored birds, and hideous intestines
hanging over the doors of houses that I hate,
and there are false teeth forgotten in a coffeepot,
there are mirrors   • mirrors only show reflections
that ought to have wept from shame and terror,
there are umbrellas everywhere, and venoms, and umbilical cords.

I stroll along serenely with my eyes, my shoes,   • Contradictions
my rage, forgetting everything,
I walk by, going through office buildings and orthopedic shops,
and courtyards with washing hanging from the line:
underwear, towels, and shirts from which slow
dirty tears are falling.   • no people in the clothes?

ROBERT BLY

15

ODA A FEDERICO GARCÍA LORCA

Si pudiera llorar de miedo en una casa sola,
si pudiera sacarme los ojos y comérmelos,
lo haría por tu voz de naranjo enlutado
y por tu poesía que sale dando gritos.

Porque por ti pintan de azul los hospitales
y crecen las escuelas y los barrios marítimos,
y se pueblan de plumas los ángeles heridos,
y se cubren de escamas los pescados nupciales,
y van volando al cielo los erizos:
por ti las sastrerías con sus negras membranas
se llenan de cucharas y de sangre,
y tragan cintas rojas, y se matan a besos,
y se visten de blanco.

Cuando vuelas vestido de durazno,
cuando ríes con risa de arroz huracanado,
cuando para cantar sacudes las arterias y los dientes,
la garganta y los dedos,
me moriría por lo dulce que eres,
me moriría por los lagos rojos
en donde en medio del otoño vives
con un corcel caído y un dios ensangrentado,
me moriría por los cementerios
que como cenicientos ríos pasan
con agua y tumbas,
de noche, entre campanas ahogadas:
ríos espesos como dormitorios
de soldados enfermos, que de súbito crecen

elegic?

ODE TO FEDERICO GARCÍA LORCA

If I could weep with fear in a solitary house,
if I could take out my eyes and eat them,
I would do it for your black-draped orange-tree voice
and for your poetry that comes forth shouting.

Because for you they paint hospitals bright blue,
and schools and sailors' quarters grow,
and wounded angels are covered with feathers,
and nuptial fish are covered with scales,
and hedgehogs go flying to the sky:
for you tailorshops with their black skins
fill up with spoons and blood,
and swallow red ribbons and kiss each other to death,
and dress in white.

When you fly dressed as a peach tree,
when you laugh with a laugh of hurricaned rice,
when to sing you shake arteries and teeth,
throat and fingers,
I could die for how sweet you are,
I could die for the red lakes
where in the midst of autumn you live
with a fallen steed and a bloodied god,
I could die for the cemeteries
that pass like ash-gray rivers
with water and tombs,
at night, among drowned bells:
rivers as thick as wards
of sick soldiers, that suddenly grow

hacia la muerte en ríos con números de mármol
y coronas podridas, y aceites funerales:
me moriría por verte de noche
mirar pasar las cruces anegadas,
de pie y llorando,
porque ante el río de la muerte lloras
abandonadamente, heridamente,
lloras llorando, con los ojos llenos
de lágrimas, de lágrimas, de lágrimas.

Si pudiera de noche, perdidamente solo,
acumular olvido y sombra y humo
sobre ferrocarriles y vapores,
con un embudo negro,
mordiendo las cenizas,
lo haría por el árbol en que creces,
por los nidos de aguas doradas que reúnes,
y por la enredadera que te cubre los huesos
comunicándote el secreto de la noche.

Ciudades con olor a cebolla mojada
esperan que tú pases cantando roncamente,
y silenciosos barcos de esperma te persiguen,
y golondrinas verdes hacen nido en tu pelo,
y además caracoles y semanas,
mástiles enrollados y cerezos
definitivamente circulan cuando asoman
tu pálida cabeza de quince ojos
y tu boca de sangre sumergida.

Si pudiera llenar de hollín las alcaldías
y, sollozando, derribar relojes,

toward death in rivers with marble numbers
and rotted crowns, and funeral oils:
I could die to see you at night
watching the sunken crosses go by,
standing and weeping,
because before death's river you weep
forlornly, woundedly,
you weep weeping, your eyes filled
with tears, with tears, with tears.

• dark images

If at night, wildly alone, I could
gather oblivion and shadow and smoke
above railroads and steamships,
with a black funnel,
biting the ashes,
I would do it for the tree in which you grow,
for the nests of golden waters that you gather,
and for the vine that covers your bones,
revealing to you the secret of the night.

Cities with a smell of wet onions
wait for you to pass singing raucously,
and silent sperm boats pursue you,
and green swallows nest in your hair,
and also snails and weeks,
furled masts and cherry trees
definitively walk about when they glimpse
your pale fifteen-eyed head
and your mouth of submerged blood.

If I could fill town halls with soot
and, sobbing, tear down clocks,

sería para ver cuándo a tu casa
llega el verano con los labios rotos,
llegan muchas personas de traje agonizante,
llegan regiones de triste esplendor,
llegan arados muertos y amapolas,
llegan enterradores y jinetes,
llegan planetas y mapas con sangre,
llegan buzos cubiertos de ceniza,
llegan enmascarados arrastrando doncellas
atravesadas por grandes cuchillos,
llegan raíces, venas, hospitales,
manantiales, hormigas,
llega la noche con la cama en donde
muere entre las arañas un húsar solitario,
llega una rosa de odio y alfileres,
llega una embarcación amarillenta,
llega un día de viento con un niño,
llego yo con Oliverio, Norah,
Vicente Aleixandre, Delia,
Maruca, Malva Marina, María Luisa y Larco,
la Rubia, Rafael Ugarte,
Cotapos, Rafael Alberti,
Carlos, Bebé, Manolo Altolaguirre,
Molinari,
Rosales, Concha Méndez,
y otros que se me olvidan.

Ven a que te corone, joven de la salud
y de la mariposa, joven puro
como un negro relámpago perpetuamente libre,
y conversando entre nosotros,
ahora, cuando no queda nadie entre las rocas,

it would be to see when to your house
comes summer with its broken lips,
come many people with dying clothes,
come regions of sad splendor,
come dead plows and poppies,
come gravediggers and horsemen,
come planets and maps with blood,
come buzzards covered with ashes,
come masked men dragging damsels
pierced by great knives,
come roots, veins, hospitals,
springs, ants,
comes night with the bed where
a solitary hussar is dying among the spiders,
comes a rose of hatred and pins,
comes a yellowish vessel,
comes a windy day with a child,
come I with Oliverio, Norah,
Vicente Aleixandre, Delia,
Maruca, Malva Marina, María Luisa, and Larco,
the Blond, Rafael Ugarte,
Cotapos, Rafael Alberti,
Carlos, Bebé, Manolo Altolaguirre,
Molinari,
Rosales, Concha Méndez,
and others that slip my mind.

Come, let me crown you, youth of health
and butterflies, youth pure
as a black lightningflash perpetually free,
and just between you and me,
now, when there is no one left among the rocks,

hablemos sencillamente como eres tú y soy yo:
para qué sirven los versos si no es para el rocío?
Para qué sirven los versos si no es para esa noche
en que un puñal amargo nos averigua, para ese día,
para ese crepúsculo, para ese rincón roto
donde el golpeado corazón del hombre se dispone a morir?

Sobre todo de noche,
de noche hay muchas estrellas,
todas dentro de un río
como una cinta junto a las ventanas
de las casas llenas de pobres gentes.

Alguien se les ha muerto, tal vez
han perdido sus colocaciones en las oficinas,
en los hospitales, en los ascensores,
en las minas,
sufren los seres tercamente heridos
y hay propósito y llanto en todas partes:
mientras las estrellas corren dentro de un río interminable
hay mucho llanto en las ventanas,
los umbrales están gastados por el llanto,
las alcobas están mojadas por el llanto
que llega en forma de ola a morder las alfombras.

Federico,
tú ves el mundo, las calles,
el vinagre,
las despedidas en las estaciones
cuando el humo levanta sus ruedas decisivas
hacia donde no hay nada sino algunas
separaciones, piedras, vías férreas.

let us speak simply, man to man:
what are verses for if not for the dew?
What are verses for if not for that night
in which a bitter dagger finds us out, for that day,
for that dusk, for that broken corner
where the beaten heart of man makes ready to die?

Above all at night,
at night there are many stars,
all within a river
like a ribbon next to the windows
of houses filled with the poor.

Someone of theirs has died, perhaps
they have lost their jobs in the offices,
in the hospitals, in the elevators,
in the mines,
human beings suffer stubbornly wounded
and there are protests and weeping everywhere:
while the stars flow within an endless river
there is much weeping at the windows,
the thresholds are worn away by the weeping,
the bedrooms are soaked by the weeping
that comes wave-shaped to bite the carpets.

Federico,
you see the world, the streets,
the vinegar,
the farewells in the stations
when the smoke lifts its decisive wheels
toward where there is nothing but some
separations, stones, railroad tracks.

Hay tantas gentes haciendo preguntas
por todas partes.
Hay el ciego sangriento, y el iracundo, y el
desanimado,
y el miserable, el árbol de las uñas,
el bandolero con la envidia a cuestas.

Así es la vida, Federico, aquí tienes
las cosas que te puede ofrece mi amistad
de melancólico varón varonil.
Ya sabes por ti mismo muchas cosas,
y otras irás sabiendo lentamente.

There are so many people asking questions
everywhere.
There is the bloody blindman, and the angry one, and the
disheartened one,
and the wretch, the thorn tree,
the bandit with envy on his back.

That's the way life is, Federico, here you have
the things that my friendship can offer you,
the friendship of a melancholy manly man.
By yourself you already know many things,
and others you will slowly get to know.

• Belief in life after   DONALD D. WALSH
   death?

FROM

Tercera residencia

Third Residence

(1934–45)

EXPLICO ALGUNAS COSAS

Preguntaréis: Y dónde están las lilas?
Y la metafísica cubierta de amapolas?
Y la lluvia que a menudo golpeaba
sus palabras llenándolas
de agujeros y pájaros?

Os voy a contar todo lo que me pasa.

Yo vivía en un barrio
de Madrid, con campanas,
con relojes, con árboles.

Desde allí se veía
el rostro seco de Castilla
como un océano de cuero.
                    Mi casa era llamada
la casa de las flores, porque por todas partes
estallaban geranios: era
una bella casa
con perros y chiquillos.
                    Raúl, te acuerdas?
Te acuerdas, Rafael?
                    Federico, te acuerdas
debajo de la tierra,
te acuerdas de mi casa con balcones en donde
la luz de junio ahogaba flores en tu boca?
                    Hermano, hermano!

I EXPLAIN A FEW THINGS

You will ask: But where are the lilacs?
And the metaphysics covered with poppies?
And the rain that often struck
his words, filling them
with holes and birds?

Let me tell you what's happening with me.

I lived in a barrio
of Madrid, with bells,
with clocks, with trees.

From there you could see
the parched face of Castile
like an ocean of leather.
                    My house was called
the house of flowers, because from everywhere
geraniums burst: it was
a beautiful house,
with dogs and children.
                    Raul, do you remember?
Do you remember, Rafael?
                    Federico, do you remember
under the ground,
do you remember my house with balconies
where the June light drowned the flowers in your mouth?
                    Brother, brother!

29

Todo
eran grandes voces, sal de mercaderías,
aglomeraciones de pan palpitante,
mercados de mi barrio de Argüelles con su estatua
como un tintero pálido entre las merluzas:
el aceite llegaba a las cucharas,
un profundo latido
de pies y manos llenaba las calles,
metros, litros, esencia
aguda de la vida,
                    pescados hacinados,
contextura de techos con sol frío en el cual
la flecha se fatiga,
delirante marfil fino de las patatas,
tomates repetidos hasta el mar.

Y una mañana todo estaba ardiendo
y una mañana las hogueras
salían de la tierra
devorando seres,
y desde entonces fuego,
pólvora desde entonces,
y desde entonces sangre.

Bandidos con aviones y con moros,
bandidos con sortijas y duquesas,
bandidos con frailes negros bendiciendo
venían por el cielo a matar niños,
y por las calles la sangre de los niños
corría simplemente, como sangre de niños.

Everything
was loud voices, salt of goods,
crowds of pulsating bread,
marketplaces in my barrio of Arguelles with its statue
like a pale inkwell set down among the hake:
oil flowed into spoons,
a deep throbbing
of feet and hands filled the streets,
meters, liters, the hard
edges of life,   *line jump?*
                heaps of fish,
geometry of roofs under a cold sun in which
the weathervane grew tired,
delirious fine ivory of potatoes,
tomatoes, more tomatoes, all the way to the sea.

And one morning it all was burning,
and one morning bonfires   *Sounds like volcano*
sprang out of the earth
devouring humans,
and from then on fire,
gunpowder from then on,
and from then on blood.

Bandidos with planes and Moors,
bandidos with rings, and duchesses,
bandidos with black friars signing the cross
coming down from the sky to kill children,
and in the streets the blood of the children
ran simply, like blood of children.

Chacales que el chacal rechazaría,
piedras que el cardo seco mordería escupiendo,
víboras que las víboras odiaran!

Frente a vosotros he visto la sangre
de España levantarse
para ahogaros en una sola ola
de orgullo y de cuchillos!

Generales
traidores:
mirad mi casa muerta,
mirad España rota:
pero de cada casa muerta sale metal ardiendo
en vez de flores,
pero de cada hueco de España
sale España,
pero de cada niño muerto sale un fusil con ojos,
pero de cada crimen nacen balas
que os hallarán un día el sitio
del corazón.

Preguntaréis por qué su poesía
no nos habla del sueño, de las hojas,
de los grandes volcanes de su país natal?

Venid a ver la sangre por las calles,
venid a ver
la sangre por las calles,
venid a ver la sangre
por las calles!

Jackals the jackals would despise,
stones the dry thistle would bite on and spit out,
vipers the vipers would abominate.

Facing you I have seen the blood
of Spain rise up
to drown you in a single wave
of pride and knives.

Traitors,
generals:
look at my dead house,
look at Spain broken:
from every house burning metal comes out   *Before + after*
instead of flowers,   *thoughts*
from every crater of Spain
comes Spain
from every dead child comes a rifle with eyes,
from every crime bullets are born
that one day will find out in you
the site of the heart.

You will ask: why doesn't his poetry
speak to us of dreams, of leaves
of the great volcanoes of his native land?

Come and see the blood in the streets,
come and see
the blood in the streets,   *different line breaks*
come and see the blood   *give it more meaning*
in the streets!

GALWAY KINNELL

No han muerto! Están en medio
de la pólvora,
de pie, como mechas ardiendo.
Sus sombras puras se han unido
en la pradera de color de cobre
como una cortina de viento blindado,
como una barrera de color de furia,
como el mismo invisible pecho del cielo.

Madres! Ellos están de pie en el trigo,
altos como el profundo mediodía,
dominando las grandes llanuras!
Son una campanada de voz negra
que a través de los cuerpos de acero asesinado
repica la victoria.
                      Hermanas como el polvo
caído, corazones
quebrantados,
tened fe en vuestros muertos!
No sólo son raíces
bajo las piedras teñidas de sangre,
no sólo sus pobres huesos derribados
definitivamente trabajan en la tierra,
sino que aun sus bocas muerden pólvora seca
y atacan como océanos de hierro, y aún
sus puños levantados contradicen la muerte.

Porque de tantos cuerpos una vida invisible
se levanta. Madres, banderas, hijos!

SONG FOR THE MOTHERS OF SLAIN MILITIAMEN

They have not died! They are in the midst
of the gunpowder,
standing, like burning wicks.
Their pure shadows have gathered
in the copper-colored meadowland
like a curtain of armored wind,
like a barricade the color of fury,
like the invisible heart of heaven itself.

Mothers! They are standing in the wheat,
tall as the depth of noon,
dominating the great plains!
They are a black-voiced bell stroke
that across the bodies murdered by steel
is ringing out victory.
                              Sisters like the fallen
dust, shattered
hearts,
have faith in your dead.
They are not only roots
beneath the bloodstained stones,
not only do their poor demolished bones
definitively till the soil,
but their mouths still bite dry powder
and attack like iron oceans, and still
their upraised fists deny death.

Because from so many bodies an invisible life
rises up. Mothers, banners, sons!

Un solo cuerpo vivo como la vida:
un rostro de ojos rotos vigila las tinieblas
con una espada llena de esperanzas terrestres!

Dejad
vuestros mantos de luto, juntad todas
vuestras lágrimas hasta hacerlas metales:
que allí golpeamos de día y de noche,
allí pateamos de día y de noche,
allí escupimos de día y de noche
hasta que caigan las puertas del odio!

Yo no me olvido de vuestras desgracias, conozco
vuestros hijos
y si estoy orgulloso de sus muertes,
estoy también orgulloso de sus vidas.
                                        Sus risas
relampagueaban en los sordos talleres,
sus pasos en el Metro
sonaban a mi lado cada día, y junto
a las naranjas de Levante, a las redes del sur, junto
a la tinta de las imprentas, sobre el cemento de las arquitecturas
he visto llamear sus corazones de fuego y energías.

Y como en vuestros corazones, madres,
hay en mi corazón tanto luto y tanta muerte
que parece una selva
mojada por la sangre que mató sus sonrisas,
y entran en él las rabiosas nieblas del desvelo
con la desgarradora soledad de los días.

A single body as alive as life:
a face of broken eyes keeps vigil in the darkness
with a sword filled with earthly hopes!

Put aside
your mantles of mourning, join all
your tears until you make them metal:
for there we strike by day and by night,
there we kick by day and by night,
there we spit by day and by night
until the doors of hatred fall!

I do not forget your misfortunes, I know
your sons,
and if I am proud of their deaths,
I am also proud of their lives.

                              Their laughter
flashed in the silent workshops,
their steps in the subway
sounded at my side each day, and next
to the oranges from the Levant, to the nets from the South, next
to the ink from the printing presses, over the cement of the
        architecture
I have seen their hearts flame with fire and energy.

And just as in your hearts, mothers,
there is in my heart so much mourning and so much death
that it is like a forest
drenched by the blood that killed their smiles,
and into it enter the rabid mists of vigilance with the rending
        loneliness of the days.

Pero
más que la maldición a las hienas sedientas, al estertor bestial
que aúlla desde el África sus patentes inmundas,
más que la cólera, más que el desprecio, más que el llanto,
madres atravesadas por la angustia y la muerte,
mirad el corazón del noble día que nace,
y sabed que vuestros muertos sonríen desde la tierra
levantando los puños sobre el trigo.

But
more than curses for the thirsty hyenas, the bestial death rattle,
that howls from Africa its filthy privileges,
more than anger, more than scorn, more than weeping,
mothers pierced by anguish and death,
look at the heart of the noble day that is born,
and know that your dead ones smile from the earth
raising their fists above the wheat.

DONALD D. WALSH

Canto general

Canto General

(1938–49)

LA UNITED FRUIT CO.

Cuando sonó la trompeta, estuvo
todo preparado en la tierra
y Jehová repartió el mundo
a Coca-Cola Inc., Anaconda,
Ford Motors, y otras entidades:
la Compañía Frutera Inc.
se reservó lo más jugoso,
la costa central de mi tierra,
la dulce cintura de América.
Bautizó de nuevo sus tierras
como «Repúblicas Bananas»
y sobre los muertos dormidos,
sobre los héroes inquietos
que conquistaron la grandeza,
la libertad y las banderas,
estableció la ópera bufa:
enajenó los albedríos,
regaló coronas de César,
desenvainó la envidia, atrajo
la dictadura de las moscas,
moscas Trujillo, moscas Tachos,
moscas Carías, moscas Martínez,
moscas Ubico, moscas húmedas
de sangre humilde y mermelada,
moscas borrachas que zumban
sobre las tumbas populares,
moscas de circo, sabias moscas
entendidas en tiranía.

UNITED FRUIT CO.

When the trumpet blared everything
on earth was prepared
and Jehovah distributed the world
to Coca-Cola Inc., Anaconda,
Ford Motors, and other entities:
United Fruit Inc.
reserved for itself the juiciest,
the central seaboard of my land,
America's sweet waist.
It rebaptized its lands
the "Banana Republics,"
and upon the slumbering corpses,
upon the restless heroes
who conquered renown,
freedom, and flags,
it established the comic opera:
it alienated self-destiny,
regaled Caesar's crowns,
unsheathed envy, drew
the dictatorship of flies:
Trujillo flies, Tacho flies,
Carías flies, Martínez flies,
Ubico flies, flies soaked
in humble blood and jam,
drunk flies that drone
over the common graves,
circus flies, clever flies
versed in tyranny.

Entre las moscas sanguinarias
la Frutera desembarca,
arrasando el café y las frutas
en sus barcos que deslizaron
como bandejas el tesoro
de nuestras tierras sumergidas.

Mientras tanto, por los abismos
azucarados de los puertos,
caían indios sepultados
en el vapor de la mañana:
un cuerpo rueda, una cosa
sin nombre, un número caído,
un racimo de fruta muerta
derramada en el pudridero.

Among the bloodthirsty flies
the Fruit Co. disembarks,
ravaging coffee and fruits
for its ships that spirit away
our submerged lands' treasures
like serving trays.

Meanwhile, in the seaports'
sugary abysses,
Indians collapsed, buried
in the morning mist:
a body rolls down, a nameless
thing, a fallen number,
a bunch of lifeless fruit
dumped in the rubbish heap.

JACK SCHMITT

America, no invoco tu nombre en vano.
Cuando sujeto al corazón la espada,
cuando aguanto en el alma la gotera,
cuando por las ventanas
un nuevo día tuyo me penetra,
soy y estoy en la luz que me produce,
vivo en la sombra que me determina,
duermo y despierto en tu esencial aurora:
dulce como las uvas, y terrible,
conductor del azúcar y el castigo,
empapado en esperma de tu especie,
amamantado en sangre de tu herencia.

AMERICA, I DO NOT INVOKE YOUR NAME IN VAIN

America, I do not invoke your name in vain.
When I hold the sword to my heart,
when I endure the leaks in my soul,
when your new day
penetrates me through the windows,
I'm of and I'm in the light that produces me,
I live in the shade that determines me,
I sleep and rise in your essential dawn,
sweet as grapes and terrible,
conductor of sugar and punishment,
soaked in the sperm of your species,
nursed on the blood of your legacy.

JACK SCHMITT

. . . Y tú, Capharnaum, que hasta los cielos
estás levantada, hasta los infiernos serás
abajada . . .

SAN LUCAS, X, 15

I

Al oeste de Colorado River
hay un sitio que amo.
Acudo allí con todo lo que palpitando
transcurre en mí, con todo
lo que fui, lo que soy, lo que sostengo.
Hay unas altas piedras rojas, el aire
salvaje de mil manos
las hizo edificadas estructuras:
el escarlata ciego subió desde el abismo
y en ellas se hizo cobre, fuego y fuerza.
América extendida como la piel del búfalo,
aérea y clara noche del galope,
allí hacia las alturas estrelladas,
bebo tu copa de verde rocío.

Sí, por agria Arizona y Wisconsin nudoso,
hasta Milwaukee levantada contra el viento y la nieve
o en los enardecidos pantanos de West Palm,
cerca de los pinares de Tacoma, en el espeso
olor de acero de tus bosques,
anduve pisando tierra madre,

. . . And thou, Capernaum, which art exalted to heaven,
shall be thrust down to hell . . .

ST. LUKE 10:15

I

West of the Colorado River
there's a place I love.
I take refuge there with everything alive
in me, with everything
that I have been, that I am, that I believe in.
Some high red rocks are there, the wild
air with its thousand hands
has turned them into human buildings.
The blind scarlet rose from the depths
and changed in these rocks to copper, fire, and energy.
America spread out like a buffalo skin,
light and transparent night of galloping,
near your high places covered with stars
I drink down your cup of green dew.

Yes, through acrid Arizona and Wisconsin full of knots,
as far as Milwaukee, raised to keep back the wind and the snow
or in the burning swamps of West Palm,
near the pine trees of Tacoma, in the thick odor
of your forests which is like steel,
I walked weighing down the mother earth,

49

hojas azules, piedras de cascada,
huracanes que temblaban como toda la música,
ríos que rezaban como los monasterios,
ánades y manzanas, tierras y aguas,
infinita quietud para que el trigo nazca.

Allí pude, en mi piedra central, extender al aire
ojos, oídos, manos, hasta oír
libros, locomotoras, nieve, luchas,
fábricas, tumbas, vegetales pasos,
y de Manhattan la luna en el navío,
el canto de la máquina que hila,
la cuchara de hierro que come tierra,
la perforadora con su golpe de cóndor
y cuanto corta, oprime, corre, cose:
seres y ruedas repitiendo y naciendo.

Amo el pequeño hogar del *farmer*. Recientes madres duermen
aromadas como el jarabe del tamarindo, las telas
recién planchadas. Arde
el fuego en mil hogares rodeados de cebollas.
(Los hombres cuando cantan cerca del río tienen
una voz ronca como las piedras del fondo:
el tabaco salió de sus anchas hojas
y como un duende del fuego llegó a estos hogares.)
Missouri adentro venid, mirad el queso y la harina,
las tablas olorosas, rojas como violines,
el hombre navegando la cebada,
el potro azul recién montado huele
el aroma del pan y de la alfalfa:
campanas, amapolas, herrerías,
y en los destartalados cinemas silvestres

blue leaves, waterfalls of stones,
hurricanes vibrating as all music does,
rivers that muttered prayers like monasteries,
geese and apples, territories and waters,
infinite silence in which the wheat could be born.

I was able there, in my deep stony core, to stretch my eyes, ears, hands,
far out into the air until I heard
books, locomotives, snow, battles,
factories, cemeteries, footsteps, plants,
and the moon on a ship from Manhattan,
the song of the machine that is weaving,
the iron spoon that eats the earth,
the drill that strikes like a condor,
and everything that cuts, presses, sews:
creatures and wheels repeating themselves and being born.

I love the farmer's small house. New mothers are asleep
with a good smell like the sap of the tamarind, clothes
just ironed. Fires are burning in a thousand homes,
with drying onions hanging around the fireplace.
(When they are singing near the river the men's voices
are deep as the stones at the river bottom;
and tobacco rose from its wide leaves
and entered these houses like a spirit of the fire.)
Come deeper into Missouri, look at the cheese and the flour,
the boards aromatic and red as violins,
the man moving like a ship among the barley,
the blue-black colt just home from a ride smells
the odor of bread and alfalfa:
bells, poppies, blacksmith shops,
and in the run-down movies in the small towns

el amor abre su dentadura
en el sueño nacido de la tierra.
Es tu paz lo que amamos, no tu máscara.
No es hermoso tu rostro de guerrero.
Eres hermosa y ancha, Norte América.
Vienes de humilde cuna como una lavandera,
junto a tus ríos, blanca.
Edificada en lo desconocido,
es tu paz de panal lo dulce tuyo.
Amamos tu hombre con las manos rojas
de barro de Oregón, tu niño negro
que te trajo la música nacida
en su comarca de marfil: amamos
tu ciudad, tu substancia,
tu luz, tus mecanismos, la energía
del Oeste, la pacífica
miel, de colmenar y aldea,
el gigante muchacho en el tractor,
la avena que heredaste
de Jefferson, la rueda rumorosa
que mide tu terrestre oceanía,
el humo de una fábrica y el beso
número mil de una colonia nueva:
tu sangre labradora es la que amamos:
tu mano popular llena de aceite.

Bajo la noche de las praderas hace ya tiempo
reposan sobre la piel del búfalo en un grave
silencio las sílabas, el canto
de lo que fui antes de ser, de lo que fuimos.
Melville es un abeto marino, de sus ramas
nace una curva de carena, un brazo

love opens its mouth full of teeth
in a dream born of the earth.
What we love is your peace, not your mask.
Your warrior's face is not handsome.
North America, you are handsome and spacious.
You come, like a washerwoman, from
a simple cradle, near your rivers, pale.
Built up from the unknown,
what is sweet in you is your hivelike peace.
We love the man with his hands red
from the Oregon clay, your Negro boy
who brought you the music born
in his country of tusks: we love
your city, your substance,
your light, your machines, the energy
of the West, the harmless
honey from hives and little towns,
the huge farm boy, on his tractor,
the oats which you inherited
from Jefferson, the noisy wheel
that measures your oceanic earth,
the factory smoke and the kiss,
the thousandth, of a new colony:
what we love is your workingman's blood:
your unpretentious hand covered with oil.

For years now under the prairie night
in a heavy silence on the buffalo skin
syllables have been asleep, poems
about what I was before I was born, what we were.
Melville is a sea fir, the curve of the keel
springs from his branches, an arm

de madera y navío. Whitman innumerable
como los cereales, Poe en su matemática
tiniebla, Dreiser, Wolfe,
frescas heridas de nuestra propia ausencia,
Lockridge reciente, atados a la profundidad,
cuántos otros, atados a la sombra:
sobre ellos la misma aurora del hemisferio arde
y de ellos está hecho lo que somos.
Poderosos infantes, capitanes ciegos,
entre acontecimientos y follajes amedrentados a veces,
interrumpidos por la alegría y por el duelo,
bajo las praderas cruzadas de tráfico,
cuántos muertos en las llanuras antes no visitadas:
inocentes atormentados, profetas recién impresos,
sobre la piel del búfalo de las praderas.

De Francia, de Okinawa, de los atolones
de Leyte (Norman Mailer lo ha dejado escrito),
del aire enfurecido y de las olas,
han regresado casi todos los muchachos.
Casi todos . . . Fue verde y amarga la historia
de barro y sudor: no oyeron
bastante el canto de los arrecifes
ni tocaron tal vez sino para morir en las islas, las coronas
de fulgor y fragancia: sangre y estiércol
los persiguieron, la mugre y las ratas,
y un cansado y desolado corazón que luchaba.
Pero ya han vuelto,

of timber and ship. Whitman impossible to count
as grain, Poe in his mathematical
darkness, Dreiser, Wolfe,
fresh wounds of our own absence,
Lockridge more recently, all bound to the depths,
how many others, bound to the darkness:
over them the same dawn of the hemisphere burns,
and out of them what we are has come.
Powerful foot soldiers, blind captains,
frightened at times among actions and leaves,
checked in their work by joy and by mourning,
under the plains crossed by traffic,
how many dead men in the fields never visited before:
innocent ones tortured, prophets only now published,
on the buffalo skin of the prairies.

From France, and Okinawa, and the atolls
of Leyte (Norman Mailer has written it out)
and the infuriated air and the waves,
almost all the men have come back now,
almost all . . . The history of mud and sweat
was green and sour; they did not hear
the singing of the reefs long enough
and perhaps never touched the islands, those wreaths of brilliance
    and perfume,
except to die: dung and blood
hounded them, the filth and the rats,
and a fatigued and ruined heart that went on fighting.
But they have come back,

              los habéis recibido
en el ancho espacio de las tierras extendidas
y se han cerrado (los que han vuelto) como una corola
de innumerables pétalos anónimos
para renacer y olvidar.

you have received them
into the immensity of the open lands
and they have closed (those who came back) like a flower
with thousands of nameless petals
to be reborn and forget.

ROBERT BLY

LA HUELGA

Extraña era la fábrica inactiva.
Un silencio en la planta, una distancia
entre máquina y hombre, como un hilo
cortado entre planetas, un vacío
de las manos del hombre que consumen
el tiempo construyendo, y las desnudas
estancias sin trabajo y sin sonido.
Cuando el hombre dejó las madrigueras
de la turbina, cuando desprendió
los brazos de la hoguera y decayeron
las entrañas del horno, cuando sacó los ojos
de la rueda y la luz vertiginosa
se detuvo en su círculo invisible,
de todos los poderes poderosos,
de los círculos puros de potencia,
de la energía sobrecogedora,
quedó un montón de inútiles aceros
y en las salas sin hombre, el aire viudo,
el solitario aroma del aceite.

Nada existía sin aquel fragmento
golpeando, sin Ramírez,
sin el hombre de ropa desgarrada.
Allí estaba la piel de los motores,
acumulada en muerto poderío,
como negros cetáceos en el fondo
pestilente de un mar sin oleaje,
o montañas hundidas de repente
bajo la soledad de los planetas.

The idle factory came to seem strange.
A silence in the plant, a distance
between machine and man, as if a thread had been cut
between two planets, an absence
of human hands that use up time
making things, and the naked
rooms without work and without noise.
When man deserted the lairs
of the turbine, when he tore off
the arms of the fire, so that the inner organs
of the furnace died, and pulled out the eyes
of the wheel, so that the dizzy light
paused in its invisible circle,
the eyes of the great energies,
of the pure circles of force,
of the stupendous power,
what remained was a heap of pointless pieces of steel,
and in the shops without men a widowed air
and the lonesome odor of oil.

Nothing existed without that fragment
hammering, without Ramírez,
without the man in torn overalls.
Nothing was left but the hides of the engines,
heaps of power gone dead,
like black whales in the polluted
depths of a sluggish sea,
or mountain ranges suddenly drowned
under the loneliness of outer space.

ROBERT BLY

FROM

Los versos del capitán

The Captain's Verses

(1951–52)

TUS MANOS

Cuando tus manos salen,
amor, hacia las mías,
qué me traen volando?
Por qué se detuvieron
en mi boca, de pronto,
por qué las reconozco
como si entonces, antes,
las hubiera tocado,
como si antes de ser
hubieran recorrido
mi frente, mi cintura?

Su suavidad venía
volando sobre el tiempo,
sobre el mar, sobre el humo,
sobre la primavera,
y cuando tú pusiste
tus manos en mi pecho,
reconocí esas alas
de paloma dorada,
reconocí esa greda
y ese color de trigo.

Los años de mi vida
yo caminé buscándolas.
Subí las escaleras,
crucé los arrecifes,
me llevaron los trenes,

YOUR HANDS

When your hands reach out
toward mine, my love,
what do they bring me flying?
Why did they
suddenly
stop at my mouth?
Why do I recognize them
as if I had
touched them
already, in the past,
as if they had journeyed
across my forehead,
my waist?

Their softness
went flying over time.
across the sea, through smoke.
over spring.
And when you placed
your hands on my chest,
I recognized a golden dove's wings,
recognized that clay
and color of wheat.

All the years of my life
I've walked in search of them.
I climbed stairs,
crossed stone-paved roads.
Trains carried me away,

las aguas me trajeron,
y en la piel de las uvas
me pareció tocarte.
La madera de pronto
me trajo tu contacto,
la almendra me anunciaba
tu suavidad secreta,
hasta que se cerraron
tus manos en mi pecho
y allí como dos alas
terminaron su viaje.

water brought me back.
And in the skin of grapes
I seemed to touch you.
Wood suddenly
brought me in contact with you,
almonds announced
your secret softness,
until your hands
closed on my chest
and, like two wings,
ended their voyage.

ILAN STAVANS

TU RISA

Quítame el pan, si quieres,
quítame el aire, pero
no me quites tu risa.

No me quites la rosa,
la lanza que desgranas,
el agua que de pronto
estalla en tu alegría,
la repentina ola
de plata que te nace.

Mi lucha es dura y vuelvo
con los ojos cansados
a veces de haber visto
la tierra que no cambia,
pero al entrar tu risa
sube al cielo buscándome
y abre para mí todas
las puertas de la vida.

Amor mío, en la hora
más oscura desgrana
tu risa, y si de pronto
ves que mi sangre mancha
las piedras de la calle,
ríe, porque tu risa
será para mis manos
como una espada fresca.

YOUR LAUGHTER

Deprive me of bread, if you want,
deprive me of air, but
don't deprive me of your laughter.

Don't deprive me of the rose,
the spear you shed the grains with,
the water splashing
swiftly in your joy,
the sudden silver wave
born in you.

My struggle is painful. As I return
with my eyes sometimes tired
from watching
the unchanging earth,
your laughter enters
and raises to heaven
in search of me,
to open
all the doors of life.

My loved one, in the darkest hour,
unsheath your laughter,
and if suddenly
you see my blood staining
the cobblestones,
laugh, for your laughter
will be for my hands
like an unsullied sword.

Junto al mar en otoño,
tu risa debe alzar
su cascada de espuma,
y en primavera, amor,
quiero tu risa como
la flor que yo esperaba,
la flor azul, la rosa
de mi patria sonora.

Ríete de la noche,
del día, de la luna,
ríete de las calles
torcidas de la isla,
ríete de este torpe
muchacho que te quiere,
pero cuando yo abro
los ojos y los cierro,
cuando mis pasos van,
cuando vuelven mis pasos,
niégame el pan, el aire,
la luz, la primavera,
pero tu risa nunca
porque me moriría.

Near the sea in autumn,
your laughter must rise
in its cascade of foam,
and in spring, my love,
I want your laughter
to be like the flower I anticipated,
the blue flower, the rose
of my resonant homeland.

Laugh at the night,
at the day, at the moon,
laugh at the twisted
streets of the island,
laugh at this clumsy
young man who loves you.
Yet when I open my eyes
and close them,
when my steps go,
when my steps return,
deny me bread, air,
light, spring,
but never your laughter
for I would die.

ILAN STAVANS

Odas elementales

Elemental Odes

(1952–54)

ODA A LA ALCACHOFA

La alcachofa
de tierno corazón
se vistió de guerrero,
erecta, construyó
una pequeña cúpula,
se mantuvo
impermeable
bajo
sus escamas,
a su lado,
los vegetales locos
se encresparon,
se hicieron
zarcillos, espadañas,
bulbos conmovedores,
en el subsuelo
durmió la zanahoria
de bigotes rojos,
la viña
resecó los sarmientos
por donde sube el vino,
la col
se dedicó
a probarse faldas,
el orégano
a perfumar el mundo,
y la dulce
alcachofa
allí en el huerto,

ODE TO THE ARTICHOKE

The tender-
hearted artichoke
dressed in its armor,
built its modest cupola
and stood
erect,
impenetrable
beneath
a lamina of leaves.
Around it,
maddened vegetables,
ruffling their leaves,
contrived
creepers, cattails,
bulbs, and tubers to astound;
beneath the ground
slept
the red-whiskered carrot;
above, the grapevine
dried its runners,
bearers of the wine;
the cabbage
preened itself,
arranging its flounces;
oregano
perfumed the world,
while the gentle
artichoke
stood proudly in the garden,

vestida de guerrero,
bruñida
como una granada,
orgullosa,
y un día
una con otra
en grandes cestos
de mimbre, caminó
por el mercado
a realizar su sueño:
la milicia.
En hileras
nunca fue tan marcial
como en la feria,
los hombres
entre las legumbres
con sus camisas blancas
eran
mariscales
de las alcachofas,
las filas apretadas,
las voces de comando,
y la detonación
de una caja que cae,
pero
entonces
viene
María
con su cesto,
escoge
una alcachofa,
no le teme,

clad in armor
burnished
to a pomegranate
glow.
And then one day,
with all the other artichokes
in willow baskets,
our artichoke
set out to market
to realize its dream:
life as a soldier.
Amid the ranks
never was it so martial
as in the fair,
white-shirted
men
among the greens
marshaled
the field
of artichokes;
close formations,
shouted commands,
and the detonation
of a falling crate.
But
look,
here comes
Maria
with her shopping basket.
Unintimidated,
she selects
our artichoke,

la examina, la observa
contra la luz como si fuera un huevo,
la compra,
la confunde
en su bolsa
con un par de zapatos,
con un repollo y una
botella
de vinagre
hasta
que entrando a la cocina
la sumerge en la olla.
Así termina
en paz
esta carrera
del vegetal armado
que se llama alcachofa,
luego
escama por escama
desvestimos
la delicia
y comemos
la pacífica pasta
de su corazón verde.

examines it, holds it to
the light as if it were an egg;
she buys it,
she drops it
in a shopping bag
that holds a pair of shoes,
a cabbage head, and one
bottle
of vinegar.
Once home
and in the kitchen
she drowns it in a pot.
And thus ends
in peace
the saga
of the armored vegetable
we call the artichoke,
as
leaf by leaf
we unsheathe
its delights
and eat
the peaceable flesh
of its green heart.

MARGARET SAYERS PEDEN

ODA AL ÁTOMO

Pequeñísima
estrella,
parecías
para siempre
enterrada
en el metal: oculto,
tu diabólico
fuego.
Un día
golpearon
en la puerta
minúscula:
era el hombre.
Con una
descarga
te desencadenaron,
viste el mundo,
saliste
por el día,
recorriste
ciudades,
tu gran fulgor llegaba
a iluminar las vidas,
eras
una fruta terrible,
de eléctrica hermosura,
venías
a apresurar las llamas
del estío,

ODE TO THE ATOM

Infinitesimal
star,
you seemed
forever
buried
in metal, hidden,
your diabolic
fire.
One day
someone knocked
at your tiny
door:
it was man.
With one
explosion
he unchained you,
you saw the world,
you came out
into the daylight,
you traveled through
cities,
your great brilliance
illuminated lives,
you were a
terrible fruit
of electric beauty,
you came to
hasten the flames
of summer,

y entonces
llegó
armado
con anteojos de tigre
y armadura,
con camisa cuadrada,
sulfúricos bigotes,
cola de puerco espín,
llegó el guerrero
y te sedujo:
duerme,
te dijo,
enróllate,
átomo, te pareces
a un dios griego,
a una primaveral
modista de París,
acuéstate
en mi uña,
entra en esta cajita,
y entonces
el guerrero
te guardó en su chaleco
como si fueras sólo
píldora
norteamericana,
y viajó por el mundo
dejándote caer
en Hiroshima.

Despertamos.

and then
wearing
a predator's eyeglasses,
armor,
and a checked shirt,
sporting sulfuric mustaches
and a prehensile tail,
came
the warrior
and seduced you:
sleep,
he told you,
curl up,
atom, you resemble
a Greek god,
a Parisian modiste
in springtime,
lie down here
on my fingernail,
climb into this little box,
and then
the warrior
put you in his jacket
as if you were nothing but
a North American
pill,
and he traveled through the world
and dropped you
on Hiroshima.

We awakened.

La aurora
se había consumido.
Todos los pájaros
cayeron calcinados.
Un olor
de ataúd,
gas de las tumbas,
tronó por los espacios.
Subió horrenda
la forma del castigo
sobrehumano,
hongo sangriento, cúpula,
humareda,
espada
del infierno.
Subió quemante el aire
y se esparció la muerte
en ondas paralelas,
alcanzando
a la madre dormida
con su niño,
al pescador del río
y a los peces,
a la panadería
y a los panes,
al ingeniero
y a sus edificios,
todo
fue polvo
que mordía,
aire
asesino.

The dawn
had been consumed.
All the birds
burned to ashes.
An odor
of coffins,
gas from tombs,
thundered through space.
The shape of punishment arose,
hideous,
superhuman,
bloody mushroom, dome,
cloud of smoke,
sword
of hell.
Burning air arose,
spreading death
on parallel waves,
reaching
the mother sleeping
with her child,
the river fisherman
and the fish,
the bakery
and the bread,
the engineer
and his buildings;
everything
was acid
dust,
assassin
air.

La ciudad
desmoronó sus últimos alvéolos,
cayó, cayó de pronto,
derribada,
podrida,
los hombres
fueron súbitos leprosos,
tomaban
la mano de sus hijos
y la pequeña mano
se quedaba en sus manos.
Así, de tu refugio,
del secreto
manto de piedra
en que el fuego dormía
te sacaron,
chispa enceguecedora,
luz rabiosa,
a destruir las vidas,
a perseguir lejanas existencias,
bajo el mar,
en el aire,
en las arenas,
en en último
recodo de los puertos,
a borrar
las semillas,
a asesinar los gérmenes,
a impedir la corola,
te destinaron, átomo,
a dejar arrasadas
las naciones,

The city
crumbled its last honeycombs
and fell, fell suddenly,
demolished,
rotten;
men
were instant lepers,
they took
their children's hand
and the little hand
fell off in theirs.
So, from your refuge
in the secret
mantle of stone
in which fire slept
they took you,
blinding spark,
raging light,
to destroy lives,
to threaten distant existences,
beneath the sea,
in the air,
on the sands,
in every twist and turn
of the ports,
to destroy
seeds,
to kill cells,
to stunt the corolla,
they destined you, atom,
to level
nations,

a convertir el amor en negra pústula,
a quemar amontonados corazones
y aniquilar la sangre.

Oh chispa loca,
vuelve
a tu mortaja,
entiérrate
en tus mantos minerales,
vuelve a ser piedra ciega,
desoye a los bandidos,
colabora
tú, con la vida, con la agricultura,
suplanta los motores,
eleva la energía,
fecunda los planetas.

Ya no tienes
secreto,
camina
entre los hombres
sin máscara
terrible,
apresurando el paso
y extendiendo
los pasos de los frutos,
separando
montañas,
enderezando ríos,
fecundando,
átomo,
desbordada

to turn love into a black pustule,
to burn heaped-up hearts
and annihilate blood.

Mad spark,
go back
to your shroud,
bury yourself
in your mineral mantle,
be blind stone once again,
ignore the outlaws,
and collaborate
with life, with growing things,
replace motors,
elevate energy,
fertilize planets.

You have no secret
now,
walk
among men
without your terrible
mask,
pick up your pace
and pace
the picking of the fruit,
parting
mountains,
straightening rivers,
making fertile,
atom,
overflowing

copa
cósmica,
vuelve
a la paz del racimo,
a la velocidad de la alegría,
vuelve al recinto
de la naturaleza,
ponte a nuestro servicio,
y en vez de las cenizas
mortales
de tu máscara,
en vez de los infiernos desatados
de tu cólera,
en vez de la amenaza
de tu terrible claridad, entréganos
tu sobrecogedora
rebeldía
para los cereales,
tu magnetismo desencadenado
para fundar la paz entre los hombres,
y así no será infierno
tu luz deslumbradora,
sino felicidad,
matutina esperanza,
contribución terrestre.

cosmic
cup,
return
to the peace of the vine,
to the velocity of joy,
return to the province
of nature,
place yourself at our service,
and instead of the fatal
ashes
of your mask,
instead of the unleashed infernos
of your wrath,
instead of the menace
of your terrible light, deliver to us
your amazing
rebelliousness
for our grain,
your unchained magnetism
to found peace among men,
and then your dazzling light
will be happiness,
not hell,
hope of morning,
gift to earth.

MARGARET SAYERS PEDEN

ODA A LA CRÍTICA

Yo escribí cinco versos:
uno verde,
otro era un pan redondo,
el tercero una casa levantándose,
el cuarto era un anillo,
el quinto verso era
corto como un relámpago
y al escribirlo
me dejó en la razón su quemadura.

Y bien, los hombres,
las mujeres,
vinieron y tomaron
la sencilla materia,
brizna, viento, fulgor, barro, madera,
y con tan poca cosa
construyeron
paredes, pisos, sueños.
En una línea de mi poesía
secaron ropa al viento.
Comieron
mis palabras,
las guardaron
junto a la cabecera,
vivieron con un verso,
con la luz que salió de mi costado.
Entonces,
llegó un crítico mudo
y otro lleno de lenguas,

ODE TO CRITICISM

I wrote five poems:
one was green,
another a round wheaten loaf,
the third was a house, abuilding,
the fourth a ring,
and the fifth was
brief as a lightning flash,
and as I wrote it,
it branded my reason.

Well, then, men
and women
came and took
my simple materials,
breeze, wind, radiance, clay, wood,
and with such ordinary things
constructed
walls, floors, and dreams.
On one line of my poetry
they hung out the wash to dry.
They ate my words
for dinner,
they kept them
by the head of their beds,
they lived with poetry,
with the light that escaped from my side.
Then
came a mute critic,
then another babbling tongues,

y otros, otros llegaron
ciegos o llenos de ojos,
elegantes algunos
como claveles con zapatos rojos,
otros estrictamente
vestidos de cadáveres,
algunos partidarios
del rey y su elevada monarquía,
otros se habían
enredado en la frente
de Marx y pataleaban en su barba,
otros eran ingleses,
sencillamente ingleses,
y entre todos
se lanzaron
con dientes y cuchillos,
con diccionarios y otras armas negras,
con citas respetables,
se lanzaron
a disputar mi pobre poesía
a las sencillas gentes
que la amaban:
y la hicieron embudos,
la enrollaron,
la sujetaron con cien alfileres,
la cubrieron con polvo de esqueleto,
la llenaron de tinta,
la escupieron con suave
benignidad de gatos,
la destinaron a envolver relojes,
la protegieron y la condenaron,
le arrimaron petróleo,

and others, many others, came,
some blind, some all-seeing,
some of them as elegant
as carnations with bright red shoes,
others as severely
clothed as corpses,
some were partisans
of the king and his exalted monarchy,
others had been snared
in Marx's brow
and were kicking their feet in his beard,
some were English,
plain and simply English,
and among them
they set out
with tooth and knife,
with dictionaries and other dark weapons,
with venerable quotes,
they set out
to take my poor poetry
from the simple folk
who loved it.
They trapped and tricked it,
they rolled it in a scroll,
they secured it with a hundred pins,
they covered it with skeleton dust,
they drowned it in ink,
they spit on it with the suave
benignity of a cat,
they used it to wrap clocks,
they protected it and condemned it,
they stored it with crude oil,

le dedicaron húmedos tratados,
la cocieron con leche,
le agregaron pequeñas piedrecitas,
fueron borrándole vocales,
fueron matándole
sílabas y suspiros,
la arrugaron e hicieron
un pequeño paquete
que destinaron cuidadosamente
a sus desvanes, a sus cementerios,
luego
se retiraron uno a uno
enfurecidos hasta la locura
porque no fui bastante
popular para ellos
o impregnados de dulce menosprecio
por mi ordinaria falta de tinieblas
se retiraron
todos
y entonces,
otra vez,
junto a mi poesía
volvieron a vivir
mujeres y hombres,
de nuevo
hicieron fuego,
construyeron casas,
comieron pan,
se repartieron la luz
y en el amor unieron
relámpago y anillo.
Y ahora,

they dedicated damp treatises to it,
they boiled it with milk,
they showered it with pebbles,
and in the process erased vowels from it,
their syllables and sighs
nearly killed it,
they crumbled it and tied it up in a
little package
they scrupulously addressed
to their attics and cemeteries,
then,
one by one, they retired,
enraged to the point of madness
because I wasn't
popular enough for them,
or saturated with mild contempt
for my customary lack of shadows,
they left,
all of them,
and then,
once again,
men and women
came to live
with my poetry,
once again
they lighted fires,
built houses,
broke bread,
they shared the light
and in love joined
the lightning flash and the ring.
And now,

perdonadme, señores,
que interrumpa este cuento
que les estoy contando
y me vaya a vivir
para siempre
con la gente sencilla.

gentlemen, if you will excuse me
for interrupting this story
I'm telling,
I am leaving to live
forever
with simple people.

MARGARET SAYERS PEDEN

ODA A CÉSAR VALLEJO

A la piedra en tu rostro,
Vallejo,
a las arrugas
de las áridas sierras
yo recuerdo en mi canto,
tu frente
gigantesca
sobre tu cuerpo frágil,
el crepúsculo negro
en tus ojos
recién desenterrados,
días aquéllos,
bruscos,
desiguales,
cada hora tenía
ácidos diferentes
o ternuras
remotas,
las llaves
de la vida
temblaban
en la luz polvorienta
de la calle,
tú volvías
de un viaje
lento, bajo la tierra,
y en la altura
de las cicatrizadas cordilleras
yo golpeaba las puertas,

ODE TO CÉSAR VALLEJO

The stone in your face,
Vallejo,
the wrinkles
of arid sierras
I remember in my song.
The gigantic
forehead
over your fragile body,
I remember,
the black sunset
just unearthed
in your eyes;
those days,
rough,
uneven,
each hour with
different acids
or remote
tenderness.
The keys of life
tremble in the dusty
light of the street.
You were coming back
from a trip,
slow, under the earth,
and, at the height of the scarred cordilleras,
I banged at the door,

que se abrieran
los muros,
que se desenrollaran
los caminos,
recién llegado de Valparaíso
me embarcaba en Marsella,
la tierra
se cortaba
como un limón fragante
en frescos hemisferios amarillos,
te quedabas
tú
allí, sujeto
a nada,
con tu vida
y tu muerte,
con tu arena
cayendo,
midiéndote
y vaciándote,
en el aire,
en el humo,
en las callejas rotas
del invierno.

Era en París, vivías
en los descalabrados
hoteles de los pobres.
España
se desangraba.
Acudíamos.

asking for walls to open up,
for roads to unravel.
I was recently arrived from Valparaíso,
about to set sail for Marseille.
The planet was cut
like a fragrant lemon
into cool yellow hemispheres.
You stayed
there,
attached to nothing,
with your life and your death,
with your falling sand,
measuring yourself
and emptying yourself
in the air,
in the smoke,
in the broken alleys
of winter.

It was in Paris. You
lived in the broken-down
hotels of poor people.
Spain
was bleeding.
We responded

Y luego
te quedaste
otra vez en el humo
y así cuando
ya no fuiste, de pronto,
no fue la tierra
de las cicatrices,
no fue
la piedra andina
la que tuvo tus huesos,
sino el humo,
la escarcha
de París en invierno.

Dos veces desterrado,
hermano mío,
de la tierra y el aire,
de la vida y la muerte,
desterrado
del Perú, de tus ríos,
ausente
de tu arcilla.
No me faltaste en vida,
sino en muerte.
Te busco
gota a gota,
polvo a polvo,
en tu tierra,
amarillo
es tu rostro,
escarpado
es tu rostro,

and then you stayed behind,
again, in the smoke.
And, suddenly,
when you were no more,
the scarring earth was no more,
and the Andean stone
that held your bones
was no more.
Only smoke
and frost
were left behind
in a Paris winter.

Twice exiled,
my brother,
from land and air,
from life and death,
exiled
from Peru, from your rivers,
absent from your own clay.
You didn't miss me in life,
only in death.
I look for you,
drop by drop,
dust to dust,
in your land.
Your face
is yellow,
your face
is steep,

estás lleno
de viejas pedrerías,
de vasijas
quebradas,
subo
las antiguas
escalinatas,
tal vez
estés perdido,
enredado
entre los hilos de oro,
cubierto
de turquesas,
silencioso,
o tal vez
en tu pueblo,
en tu raza,
grano
de maíz extendido,
semilla
de bandera.
Tal vez, tal vez ahora
transmigres
y regreses,
vienes
al fin
de viaje,
de manera
que un día
te verás en el centro
de tu patria,

you are filled
with precious stones,
with broken
vessels.
I climb
ancient
stairways
Maybe I'm lost,
entangled
in threads of gold,
covered with turquoise jewels,
silent.
Or maybe
I'm in your pueblo,
in your race,
in your scattered corn,
a seed
of flag.
Maybe, maybe now
you'll
transmigrate
and return.
You're
at the end
of the journey,
so you'll find yourself
at the heart of your
homeland,

insurrecto,
viviente,
cristal de tu cristal, fuego en tu fuego,
rayo de piedra púrpura.

in rebellion,
alive,
crystal in your own crystal, fire in your own fire,
ray of purple stone.

ILAN STAVANS

FROM

Nuevas odas
elementales

New Elemental
Odes

(1955)

ODA AL DICCIONARIO

Lomo de buey, pesado
cargador, sistemático
libro espeso:
de joven
te ignoré, me vistió
la suficiencia
y me creí repleto,
y orondo como un
melancólico sapo
dictaminé: "Recibo
las palabras
directamente
del Sinaí bramante.
Reduciré
las formas a la alquimia.
Soy mago."

El gran mago callaba.

El Diccionario,
viejo y pesado, con su chaquetón
de pellejo gastado,
se quedó silencioso
sin mostrar sus probetas.

Pero un día,
después de haberlo usado
y desusado,
después

ODE TO THE DICTIONARY

Back like an ox, beast of
burden, orderly
thick book:
as a youth
I ignored you,
wrapped in my smugness,
I thought I knew it all,
and as puffed up as a
melancholy toad
I proclaimed: "I receive
my words
in a loud, clear voice
directly from Mt. Sinai.
I shall convert
forms to alchemy.
I am the Magus."

The Great Magus said nothing.

The Dictionary,
old and heavy in its scruffy
leather jacket,
sat in silence,
its resources unrevealed.

But one day,
after I'd used it
and abused it,
after

de declararlo
inútil y anacrónico camello,
cuando por largos meses, sin protesta,
me sirvió de sillón
y de almohada,
se rebeló y plantándose
en mi puerta
creció, movió sus hojas
y sus nidos,
movió la elevación de su follaje:
árbol
era,
natural,
generoso
manzano, manzanar o manzanero,
y las palabras
brillaban en su copa inagotable,
opacas o sonoras,
fecundas en la fronda del lenguaje,
cargadas de verdad y de sonido.

Aparto una
sola de
sus
páginas:
Caporal
Capuchón
qué maravilla

pronunciar estas sílabas
con aire,
y más abajo

I'd called it
useless, an anachronistic camel,
when for months, without protest,
it had served me as a chair
and a pillow,
it rebelled and planting its feet
firmly in my doorway,
expanded, shook its leaves
and nests,
and spread its foliage:
it was
a tree,
a natural,
bountiful
apple blossom, apple orchard, apple tree,
and words
glittered in its infinite branches,
opaque or sonorous,
fertile in the fronds of language,
charged with truth and sound.

I
turn
its
pages:
caporal,
capote,
what a marvel

to pronounce these plosive
syllables,
and further on,

Cápsula
hueca, esperando aceite o ambrosía,
y junto a ellas
Captura Capucete Capuchina
Caprario Captatorio
palabras
que se deslizan como suaves uvas
o que a la luz estallan
como gérmenes ciegos que esperaron
en las bodegas del vocabulario
y viven otra vez y dan la vida:
una vez más el corazón las quema.

Diccionario, no eres
tumba, sepulcro, féretro,
túmulo, mausoleo,
sino preservación,
fuego escondido,
plantación de rubíes,
perpetuidad viviente
de la esencia,
granero del idioma.
Y es hermoso
recoger en tus filas
la palabra
de estirpe,
la severa
y olvidada
sentencia,
hija de España,
endurecida
como reja de arado,

capsule,
unfilled, awaiting ambrosia or oil
and others,
capsicum, caption, capture,
comparison, capricorn,
words
as slippery as smooth grapes,
words exploding in the light
like dormant seeds waiting
in the vaults of vocabulary,
alive again, and giving life:
once again the heart distills them.

Dictionary, you are not a
tomb, sepulcher, grave,
tumulus, mausoleum,
but guard and keeper,
hidden fire,
groves of rubies,
living eternity
of essence,
depository of language.
How wonderful
to read in your columns
ancestral
words,
the severe and
long-forgotten
maxim,
daughter of Spain,
petrified
as a plow blade,

fija en su límite
de anticuada herramienta,
preservada
con su hermosura exacta
y su dureza de medalla.
O la otra
palabra
que allí vimos perdida
entre renglones
y que de pronto
se hizo sabrosa y lisa en nuestra boca
como una almendra
o tierna como un higo.

Diccionario, una mano
de tus mil manos, una
de tus mil esmeraldas,
una
sola
gota
de tus vertientes virginales,
un grano
de
tus
magnánimos graneros
en el momento
justo
a mis labios conduce,
al hilo de mi pluma,
a mi tintero.
De tu espesa y sonora
profundidad de selva,

as limited in use
as an antiquated tool,
but preserved
in the precise beauty and
immutability of a medallion.
Or another
word
we find hiding
between the lines
that suddenly seems
as delicious and smooth on the tongue
as an almond,
or tender as a fig.

Dictionary, let one hand
of your thousand hands, one
of your thousand emeralds,
a
single
drop
of your virginal springs,
one grain
from
your
magnanimous granaries,
fall
at the perfect moment
upon my lips,
onto the tip of my pen,
into my inkwell.
From the depths of your
dense and reverberating jungle

dame,
cuando lo necesite,
un solo trino, el lujo
de una abeja,
un fragmento caído
de tu antigua madera perfumada
por una eternidad de jazmineros,
una
sílaba,
un temblor, un sonido,
una semilla:
de tierra soy y con palabras canto.

grant me,
at the moment it is needed,
a single birdsong, the luxury
of one bee,
one splinter
of your ancient wood perfumed
by an eternity of jasmine,
one
syllable,
one tremor, one sound,
one seed:
I am of the earth and with words I sing.

MARGARET SAYERS PEDEN

ODA AL OJO

Poderoso eres, pero
una arenilla,
una pata de mosca,
la mitad de un miligramo
de polvo
entró en tu ojo derecho
y el mundo
se hizo negro y borroso,
las calles
se volvieron escaleras,
los edificios se cubrieron de humo,
tu amor, tu hijo, tu plato
cambiaron de color, se transformaron
en palmeras o arañas.

Cuida el ojo!

El ojo,
globo de maravilla,
pequeño
pulpo de nuestro abismo
que extrae
la luz de las tinieblas,
perla
elaboradora,
magnético
azabache,
maquinita
rápida

ODE TO THE EYE

Powerful—
but a grain of sand,
a fly's foot,
half a milligram
of dust
entered your right eye
and the world
became dark and foggy.
Streets
became staircases,
buildings were covered with smoke,
your love, your son, your dinner plate
changed color,
turning
into palm trees or spiders.

Protect the eye!

The eye,
bubble of wonder,
small
octopus of our emptiness
extracting
brightness from shade,
polished
pearl,
alluring
blackness of the sea,
swift

como nada o como nadie,
fotógrafo
vertiginoso,
pintor francés,
revelador de asombro.
Ojo,
diste nombre
a la luz de la esmeralda,
sigues
el crecimiento
del naranjo
y controlas
las leyes de la aurora,
mides,
adviertes el peligro,
te encuentras con el rayo
de otros ojos
y arde en el corazón la llamarada,
como un
milenario molusco,
te sobrecoges
al ataque del ácido,
lees,
lees
números de banqueros,
alfabetos
de tiernos colegiales de Turquía,
de Paraguay, de Malta,
lees
nóminas
y novelas,

engine
like nothing and no one,
dizzying
photographer,
French painter,
revelator of oracle.
Eye,
you name
the emerald glow,
trace
the growth
of an orange tree,
control
the laws of sunrise.
You measure,
announce danger,
encounter the glimmer
of others.
And fire burns in the heart,
like
an ancient mollusk.
You sneer
at the attacking acid.
You read,
read
the banker's numbers,
ABCs
by tender students from Turkey,
Paraguay, Malta.
Read
reports
and novels,

abarcas olas, ríos,
geografías,
exploras,
reconoces
tu bandera
en el remoto mar, entre los barcos,
guardas al náufrago
el retrato
más azul del cielo
y de noche
tu pequeña
ventana
que se cierra
se abre por otro lado como un túnel
a la indecisa patria de los sueños.

Yo vi un muerto
en la pampa
salitrera,
era
un hombre del salitre,
hermano de la arena.
En una huelga
mientras
comía
con sus compañeros
lo derribaron, luego

seize waves, rivers,
geographies.
Explorer,
you sight
your flag
in the remote sea, among the ships,
giving the shipwrecked sailor
the bluest portrait
of the sky.
Then, at night,
your small
closing
window
opens up from the other end, like a tunnel,
to the unsettled homeland of dreams.

I saw a dead man
in the salt
pampa,
a man
made of salt,
a brother of sand.
During a strike,
while
he ate
with his compañeros,
he was struck down.

en su sangre
que otra vez
volvía a las arenas,
los hombres
empaparon
sus banderas
y por la dura pampa
caminaron
cantando
y desafiando a sus verdugos.
Yo me incliné
para tocar su rostro
y en las pupilas
muertas,
retratada,
profunda,
vi
que se había quedado
viviente
su bandera,
la misma que llevaban
al combate
sus hermanos
cantando,
allí
como en el pozo
de toda
la eternidad humana
vi

So they
soaked
their flags
in his blood,
coming back to the sand.
Across the arid pampa
they walked,
singing,
defying their oppressors.
I bent down
to touch his face.
In his dead
pupils,
I saw,
photographed
in their depth,
that his flag
was still moving,
the same one taken
by his brothers
into battle
while they sang.
There,
in the
well
that holds
humankind
forever,
I saw

su bandera
como fuego escarlata,
como una amapola
indestructible.

Ojo,
tú faltabas
en mi canto
y cuando una vez más hacia el océano
fui a dirigir las cuerdas de mi lira
y de mi oda,
tú delicadamente
me mostraste
qué tonto soy: vi la vida, la tierra,
todo
lo vi,
menos mis ojos.
Entonces
dejaste penetrar
bajo mis párpados
un átomo de polvo.
Se me nubló la vista.
Vi el mundo
ennegrecido.
El oculista
detrás de una escafandra
me dirigió su rayo
y me dejó caer
como a una ostra
una gota de infierno.

his flag,
like scarlet fire,
an indestructible
poppy.

Eye,
you were missing
from his song.
When I returned to the ocean
I played my lyre's chords once again
and sang my ode.
You showed me,
delicately,
how foolish I am: I saw life, I saw the earth,
I saw
everything—
except my own eyes.
Then
you let a particle of dust
hide behind my eyelids.
I lost my sight.
I saw the world grow
darker.
The eye doctor,
in his white uniform,
pointed his ray at me.
He allowed an infernal drop
to fall
down
like an oyster.

Más tarde,
reflexivo,
recobrando la vista y admirando
los pardos, espaciosos
ojos de la que adoro,
borré mi ingratitud con esta oda
que tus
desconocidos ojos
leen.

Later,
reflexive,
having recovered my sight—and admiring
the brownish, spacious eyes
of my beloved—
I erased my ingratitude with this ode,
now being read,
mysteriously,
by you.

ILAN STAVANS

ODA A WALT WHITMAN

Yo no recuerdo
a qué edad,
ni dónde,
si en el gran Sur mojado
o en la costa
temible, bajo el breve
grito de las gaviotas,
toqué una mano y era
la mano de Walt Whitman:
pisé la tierra
con los pies desnudos,
anduve sobre el pasto,
sobre el firme rocío
de Walt Whitman.

Durante
mi juventud
toda
me acompañó esa mano,
ese rocío,
su firmeza de pino patriarca, su extensión de pradera,
y su misión de paz circulatoria.

Sin
desdeñar
los dones
de la tierra,
la copiosa
curva del capitel,

ODE TO WALT WHITMAN

I don't remember
at what age,
or where,
in the great wet South
or in the fearsome
coast, under the brief
scream of seagulls,
I touched a hand and it was
Walt Whitman's hand:
I stepped on soil
with bare feet,
I walked on grass,
on Walt Whitman's
firm dew.

During
my whole youth,
that hand accompanied me,
its dew,
the firmness of its patriarchal pine,
its broadness of prairies,
its mission of circulatory peace.

Without
rejecting
the earth's gifts,
the spire's
copious curve,

ni la inicial
purpúrea
de la sabiduría,
tu
me enseñaste
a ser americano,
levantaste
mis ojos
a los libros,
hacia
el tesoro
de los cereales:
ancho,
en la claridad
de las llanuras,
me hiciste ver
el alto
monte
tutelar. Del eco
subterráneo,
para mí
recogiste
todo,
todo lo que nacía,
cosechaste
galopando en la alfalfa,
cortando para mí las amapolas,
visitando
los ríos,
acudiendo en la tarde
a las cocinas.

or the initial
purple
wisdom,
you taught me
how to be an American.
You lifted
my eyes
to books,
toward the treasure of grain:
wide,
in the clarity
of plains,
you made me
see the soaring,
tutelary mountain.
From the subterranean
echo,
you collected
everything
for me,
everything born
you harvested
galloping in the alfalfa,
gathering poppies for me,
visiting
rivers,
appearing in kitchens
in the afternoon.

Pero no sólo
tierra
sacó a la luz
tu pala;
desenterraste
al hombre,
y el
esclavo
humillado
contigo, balanceando
la negra dignidad de su estatura,
caminó conquistando
la alegría.

Al fogonero,
abajo,
en la caldera,
mandaste
un canastito
de frutillas,
a todas las esquinas de tu pueblo
un verso
tuyo llegó de visita
y era como un trozo
de cuerpo limpio
el verso que llegaba,
como
tu propia barba pescadora
o el solemne camino de tus piernas de acacia.

Pasó entre los soldados
tu silueta

Not only did your shovel
bring earth to light;
you unearthed
man
and the
humiliated slave,
maligned like you,
balancing the black dignity
of his height,
walking in the conquest
of happiness.

To the stoker,
in the engine room
bellow,
you sent
a little basket
filled with fruit.
To all corners of your land,
your verse
traveled for a visit;
it was like a piece
of clean body,
your migrating verse,
like
your own fisherman's beard
or the solemn road of your acacia legs.

Your bard's silhouette
passed among the soldiers,

de bardo, de enfermero,
de cuidador nocturno
que conoce
el sonido
de la respiración en la agonía
y espera con la aurora
el silencioso
regreso
de la vida.

Buen panadero!
Primo hermano mayor
de mis raíces,
cupula
de araucaria,
hace
ya
cien
años
que sobre el pasto tuyo
y sus germinaciones,
el viento
pasa
sin gastar tus ojos.

Nuevos
y crueles años en tu patria:
persecuciones,
lágrimas,
prisiones,
armas envenenadas
y guerras iracundas,

the nurse,
the night watchman
who knows
the sound
of agony's dying breath
and waits with daybreak
for the quiet
return
of life.

Good baker!
My older cousin
of the same lineage,
cupola
of araucaria pine,
it's
a hundred
years
already
since wind
blew
over your grass
without
diminishing your eyes.

New
and cruel years in your homeland:
persecutions, tears,
prisons,
poisoned weapons
and furious wars

no han aplastado
la hierba de tu libro,
el manantial vital
de su frescura.
Y, ay!
los
que asesinaron
a Lincoln
ahora
se acuestan en su cama,
derribaron
su sitial
de olorosa madera
y erigieron un trono
por desventura y sangre
salpicado.

Pero
canta en
las estaciones
suburbanas
tu voz,
en
los
desembarcaderos
vespertinos
chapotea
como
un agua oscura

haven't smashed
the grass of your book,
the vital well
of your freshness.
And, ay!
those who killed
Lincoln
now
lie in his bed.
They brought down
his seat of honor,
made of fragrant wood,
instead raising a throne
sprinkled with
misbegotten
blood.

But
your voice
sings
in the suburban
stations,
your word
dabbles
in the afternoon
ports
like
dark water,

tu palabra,
tu pueblo
blanco
y negro,
pueblo
de pobres,
pueblo simple
como
todos
los pueblos,
no olvida
tu campana:
se congrega cantando
bajo
la magnitud
de tu espaciosa vida:
entre los pueblos con tu amor camina
acariciando
el desarrollo puro
de la fraternidad sobre la tierra.

your people,
black and white,
in poverty,
your people,
like
all people,
won't forget
your bell:
they
congregate
singing
under the magnitude
of your
spacious life:
your love walks
among them,
caressing
the clean growth
of humankind on earth.

ILAN STAVANS

Tercer libro de odas

Third Book of Odes

(1955–57)

ODA A LA SAL

Esta sal
del salero
yo la vi en los salares.
Sé que
no
van a creerme,
pero
canta,
canta la sal, la piel
de los salares,
canta
con una boca ahogada
por la tierra.
Me estremecí en aquellas
soledades
cuando escuché
la voz
de
la sal
en el desierto.
Cerca de Antofagasta
toda
la pampa salitrosa
suena:
es una
voz
quebrada,
un lastimero
canto.

ODE TO SALT

In the salt mines
I saw the salt
in this shaker.
I know you won't believe me,
but there
it sings,
the salt sings, the skin
of the salt mines
sings
with a mouth choking
on dirt.
Alone
when I heard
the voice
of salt,
I trembled
in the empty
desert.
Near Antofagasta
the whole
salted plain
shouts out
in its
cracked
voice
a pitiful
song.

Luego en sus cavidades
la sal gema, montaña
de una luz enterrada,
catedral transparente,
cristal del mar, olvido
de las olas.

Y luego en cada mesa
de ese mundo,
sal,
tu substancia
ágil
espolvoreando
la luz vital
sobre
los alimentos.
Preservadora
de las antiguas
bodegas del navío,
descubridora
fuiste
en el océano,
materia
adelantada
en los desconocidos, entreabiertos
senderos de la espuma.

Polvo del mar, la lengua
de ti recibe un beso
de la noche marina:

Then in its caverns
jewels of rock salt, a mountain
of light buried under earth,
transparent cathedral,
crystal of the sea, oblivion
of the waves.

And now on each table
of the world
your agile
essence,
salt,
spreading
a vital luster
on
our food.
Preserver
of the ancient
stores in the holds
of ships, you were
the explorer
of the seas,
matter
foretold
in the secret, half-open
trails of foam.

Dust of water, the tongue
receives through you a kiss
from the marine night:

el gusto funde en cada
sazonado manjar tu oceanía
y así la mínima,
la minúscula
ola del salero
nos enseña
no sólo su doméstica blancura,
sino el sabor central del infinito.

taste melds
your oceanity
into each rich morsel
and thus the least
wave
of the saltshaker
teaches us
not merely domestic purity
but also the essential flavor of the infinite.

PHILIP LEVINE

FROM

Estravagario

Extravagaria

(1957–58)

PIDO SILENCIO

Ahora me dejen tranquilo.
Ahora se acostumbren sin mí.

Yo voy a cerrar los ojos.

Y sólo quiero cinco cosas,
cinco raíces preferidas.

Una es el amor sin fin.

Lo segundo es ver el otoño.
No puedo ser sin que las hojas
vuelen y vuelvan a la tierra.

Lo tercero es el grave invierno,
la lluvia que amé, la caricia
del fuego en el frío silvestre.

En cuarto lugar el verano
redondo como una sandía.

La quinta cosa son tus ojos.
Matilde mía, bienamada,
no quiero dormir sin tus ojos,
no quiero ser sin que me mires:
yo cambio la primavera
por que tú me sigas mirando.

I ASK FOR SILENCE

Now they can leave me in peace,
and grow used to my absence.

I am going to close my eyes.

I only want five things,
five chosen roots.

One is an endless love.

Two is to see the autumn.
I cannot exist without leaves
flying and falling to earth.

The third is the solemn winter,
the rain I loved, the caress
of fire in the rough cold.

My fourth is the summer,
plump as a watermelon.

And fifthly, your eyes.
Matilde, my dear love,
I will not sleep without your eyes,
I will not exist but in your gaze.
I adjust the spring
for you to follow me with your eyes.

Amigos, eso es cuanto quiero.
Es casi nada y casi todo.

Ahora si quieren se vayan.

He vivido tanto que un día
tendrán que olvidarme por fuerza,
borrándome de la pizarra:
mi corazón fue interminable.

Pero porque pido silencio
no crean que voy a morirme:
me pasa todo lo contrario:
sucede que voy a vivirme.

Sucede que soy y que sigo.

No será, pues, sino que adentro
de mí crecerán cereales,
primero los granos que rompen
la tierra para ver la luz,
pero la madre tierra es oscura:
y dentro de mí soy oscuro:
soy como un pozo en cuyas aguas
la noche deja sus estrellas
y sigue sola por el campo.

Se trata de que tanto he vivido
que quiero vivir otro tanto.

That, friends, is all I want.
Next to nothing, close to everything.

Now they can go if they wish.

I have lived so much that someday
they will have to forget me forcibly,
rubbing me off the blackboard.
My heart was inexhaustible.

But because I ask for silence,
don't think I'm going to die.
The opposite is true;
it happens I'm going to live.

To be, and to go on being.

I will not be, however, if, inside me,
the crop does not keep sprouting,
the shoots first, breaking through the earth
to reach the light;
but the mothering earth is dark,
and, deep inside me, I am dark.
I am a well in the water of which
the night leaves stars behind
and goes on alone across fields.

It's a question of having lived so much
that I want to live that much more.

Nunca me sentí tan sonoro,
nunca he tenido tantos besos.

Ahora, como siempre, es temprano.
Vuela la luz con sus abejas.

Déjenme solo con el día.
Pido permiso para nacer.

I never felt my voice so clear,
never have been so rich in kisses.

Now, as always, it is early.
The light is a swarm of bees.

Let me alone with the day.
I ask leave to be born.

ALASTAIR REID

CUÁNTO PASA EN UN DÍA

Dentro de un día nos veremos.

Pero en un día crecen cosas,
se venden uvas en la calle,
cambia la piel de los tomates,
la muchacha que te gustaba
no volvió más a la oficina.

Cambiaron de pronto el cartero.
Las cartas ya no son las mismas.
Varias hojas de oro y es otro:
este árbol es ahora un rico.

Quién nos diría que la tierra
con su vieja piel cambia tanto?
Tiene más volcanes que'ayer,
el cielo tiene nuevas nubes,
los ríos van de otra manera.
Además cuánto se construye!
Yo he inaugurado centenares
de carreteras, de edificios,
de puentes puros y delgados
como navíos o violines.

Por eso cuando te saludo
y beso tu boca florida
nuestros besos son otros besos
y nuestras bocas otras bocas.

HOW MUCH HAPPENS IN A DAY

In the course of a day we shall meet one another.

But, in one day, things spring to life —
they sell grapes in the street,
tomatoes change their skin,
the young girl you wanted
never came back to the office.

They changed the postman suddenly.
The letters now are not the same.
A few golden leaves and it's different;
this tree is now well off.

Who would have said that the earth
with its ancient skin would change so much?
It has more volcanoes than yesterday,
the sky has brand-new clouds,
the rivers are flowing differently.
Besides, so much has come into being!
I have inaugurated hundreds
of highways and buildings,
delicate, clean bridges
like ships or violins.

And so, when I greet you
and kiss your flowering mouth,
our kisses are other kisses,
our mouths are other mouths.

Salud, amor, salud por todo
lo que cae y lo que florece.

Salud por ayer y por hoy,
por anteayer y por mañana.

Salud por el pan y la piedra,
salud por el fuego y la lluvia.

Por lo que cambia, nace, crece,
se consume y vuelve a ser beso.

Salud por lo que tenemos de aire
y lo que tenemos de tierra.

Cuando se seca nuestra vida
nos quedan sólo las raíces
y el viento es frío como el odio.

Entonces cambiamos de piel,
de uñas, de sangre, de mirada,
y tú me besas y yo salgo
a vender luz por los caminos.

Salud por la noche y el día
y las cuatro estaciones del alma.

Joy, my love, joy in all things,
in what falls and what flourishes.

Joy in today and yesterday,
the day before and tomorrow.

Joy in bread and stone,
joy in fire and rain.

In what changes, is born, grows,
consumes itself, and becomes a kiss again.

Joy in the air we have,
and in what we have of earth.

When our life dries up,
only the roots remain to us,
and the wind is cold like hate.

Then let us change our skin,
our nails, our blood, our gazing;
and you kiss me and I go out
to sell light on the roads.

Joy in the night and the day,
and the four stations of the soul.

ALASTAIR REID

MUCHOS SOMOS

De tantos hombres que soy, que somos,
no puedo encontrar a ninguno:
se me pierden bajo la ropa,
se fueron a otra ciudad.

Cuando todo está preparado
para mostrarme inteligente
el tonto que llevo escondido
se toma la palabra en mi boca.

Otras veces me duermo en medio
de la sociedad distinguida
y cuando busco en mí al valiente,
un cobarde que no conozco
corre a tomar con mi esqueleto
mil deliciosas precauciones.

Cuando arde una casa estimada
en vez del bombero que llamo
se precipita el incendiario
y ése soy yo. No tengo arreglo.
Qué debo hacer para escogerme?

Cómo puedo rehabilitarme?
Todos los libros que leo
celebran héroes refulgentes
siempre seguros de sí mismos:
me muero de envidia por ellos,
y en los filmes de vientos y balas

Of the many men who I am, who we are,
I can't find a single one;
they disappear among my clothes,
they've left for another city.

When everything seems to be set
to show me off as intelligent,
the fool I always keep hidden
takes over all that I say.

At other times, I'm asleep
among distinguished people,
and when I look for my brave self,
a coward unknown to me
rushes to cover my skeleton
with a thousand fine excuses.

When a decent house catches fire,
instead of the fireman I summon,
an arsonist bursts on the scene,
and that's me. What can I do?
What can I do to distinguish myself?
How can I pull myself together?

All the books I read
are full of dazzling heroes,
always sure of themselves.
I die with envy of them;
and in films full of wind and bullets,

me quedo envidiando al jinete,
me quedo admirando al caballo.

Pero cuando pido al intrépido
me sale el viejo perezoso,
y así yo no sé quién soy,
no sé cuántos soy o seremos.
Me gustaría tocar un timbre
y sacar el mí verdadero
porque si yo me necesito
no debo desaparecerme.

Mientras escribo estoy ausente
y cuando vuelvo ya he partido:
voy a ver si a las otras gentes
les pasa lo que a mí me pasa,
si son tantos como soy yo,
si se parecen a sí mismos
y cuando lo haya averiguado
voy a aprender tan bien las cosas
que para explicar mis problemas
les hablaré de geografía.

I goggle at the cowboys,
I even admire the horses.

But when I call for a hero,
out comes my lazy old self;
so I never know who I am,
nor how many I am or will be.
I'd love to be able to touch a bell
and summon the real me,
because if I really need myself,
I mustn't disappear.

While I am writing, I'm far away;
and when I come back, I've gone.
I would like to know if others
go through the same things that I do,
have as many selves as I have,
and see themselves similarly;
and when I've exhausted this problem,
I'm going to study so hard
that when I explain myself,
I'll be talking geography.

ALASTAIR REID

167

TESTAMENTO DE OTOÑO

El poeta entra a contar su condición y predilecciones

Entre morir y no morir
me decidí por la guitarra
y en esta intensa profesión
mi corazón no tiene tregua,
porque donde menos me esperan
yo llegaré con mi equipaje
a cosechar el primer vino
en los sombreros del otoño.

Entraré si cierran la puerta
y si me reciben me voy,
no soy de aquellos navegantes
que se extravían en el hielo:
yo me acomodo como el viento,
con las hojas más amarillas,
con los capítulos caídos
de los ojos de las estatuas
y si en alguna parte descanso
es en la propia nuez del fuego,
en lo que palpita y crepita
y luego viaja sin destino.

A lo largo de los renglones
habrás encontrado tu nombre,
lo siento muchísimo poco,
no se trataba de otra cosa
sino de muchísimas más,

AUTUMN TESTAMENT

The poet talks of his state and his predilections

Between dying and not dying
I picked on the guitar
and in that dedication
my heart takes no respite,
for where I'm least expected
I turn up with my stuff
to gather the first wine
in the sombreros of autumn.

If they close the door, I'll go in;
if they greet me, I'll be off.
I'm not one of those sailors
who flounder about on the ice.
I'm adaptable as the wind is,
with the yellowest leaves,
with the fallen histories
in the eyes of statues,
and if I come to rest anywhere,
it's in the nub of the fire,
the throbbing crackling part
that flies off to nowhere.

Along the margins
you'll have come across your name;
I don't apologize,
it had to do with nothing
except almost everything,

porque eres y porque no eres
y esto le pasa a todo el mundo,
nadie se da cuenta de todo
y cuando se suman las cifras
todos éramos falsos ricos:
ahora somos nuevos pobres.

Habla de sus enemigos y les participa su herencia

He sido cortado en pedazos
por rencorosas alimañas
que parecían invencibles.
Yo me acostumbré en el mar
a comer pepinos de sombra,
extrañas variedades de ámbar
y a entrar en ciudades perdidas
con camiseta y armadura
de tal manera que te matan
y tú te mueres de la risa.

Dejo pues a los que ladraron
mis pestañas de caminante,
mi predilección por la sal,
la dirección de mi sonrisa
para que todo lo lleven
con discreción, si son capaces:
ya que no pudieron matarme
no puedo impedirles después
que no se vistan con mi ropa,
que no aparezcan los domingos
con trocitos de mi cadáver,
certeramente disfrazados.

for you do and you don't exist—
that happens to everybody—
nobody realizes,
and when they add up the figures,
we're not rich at all—
now we're the new poor.

He speaks of his enemies and divides up his possessions

I've been ripped apart
by a set of spitting rodents
who seemed too much for me.
In the sea I would often eat
dark sea cucumbers,
strange kinds of amber,
and storm lost cities
in my shirt and my armor
in ways that would kill you—
you would die of laughter.

So I leave to all who snarled at me
my traveler's eyelashes,
my passion for salt,
the slant of my smile—
let them take it all away
discreetly, if that's possible;
since they weren't able to kill me
I can hardly stop them
from dressing in my clothes
or appearing on Sundays
convincingly disguised.

Si no dejé tranquilo a nadie
no me van a dejar tranquilo,
y se verá y eso no importa:
publicarán mis calcetines.

Se dirige a otros sectores

Dejé mis bienes terrenales
a mi Partido y a mi pueblo,
ahora se trata de otras cosas,
cosas tan oscuras y claras
que son sin embargo una sola.
Así sucede con las uvas,
y sus dos poderosos hijos,
el vino blanco, el vino rojo,
toda la vida es roja y blanca,
toda claridad es oscura,
y no todo es tierra y adobe,
hay en mi herencia sombra y sueños.

Contesta a algunos bien intencionados

Me preguntaron una vez
por qué escribía tan oscuro,
pueden preguntarlo a la noche,
al mineral, a las raíces.
Yo no supe qué contestar
hasta que luego y después
me agredieron dos desalmados
acusándome de sencillo:
que responda el agua que corre,
y me fui corriendo y cantando.

I left no one in peace
so they'll grant me no peace.
That's clear, but it doesn't matter —
they'll be publishing my socks.

He turns to other matters

I've left my worldly goods
to my party and my people —
we're talking here of other things,
things both obscure and clear
which all add up to one thing.
It's the same with the grapes
and their two powerful children,
white wine, red wine.
All life is red and white,
all clarity is cloudy.
It's not all earth and adobe —
I inherited shadows and dreams.

He replies to some well-meaning people

Once they asked me
why my writing was so obscure.
They might ask the night that,
or minerals, or roots.
I didn't know what to answer,
then, some time after,
two crazy men attacked me,
saying I was simple —
the answer's in running water
and I went off, running and singing.

Destina sus penas

A quién dejo tanta alegría
que pululó por mis venas
y este ser y no ser fecundo
que me dio la naturaleza?
He sido un largo río lleno
de piedras duras que sonaban
con sonidos claros de noche,
con cantos oscuros de día
y a quién puedo dejarle tanto,
tanto que dejar y tan poco,
una alegría sin objeto,
un caballo solo en el mar,
un telar que tejía viento?

Dispone de sus regocijos

Mis tristezas se las destino
a los que me hicieron sufrir,
pero me olvidé cuáles fueron,
y no sé dónde las dejé,
si las ven en medio del bosque
son como las enredaderas:
suben del suelo con sus hojas
y terminan donde terminas,
en tu cabeza o en el aire,
y para que no suban más
hay que cambiar de primavera.

He parcels out his sufferings

Has anyone been granted
as much joy as I have
(it flows through my veins)
and this fruitful unfruitful mixture
that is my nature?
I've been a great flowing river
with hard ringing stones,
with clear night-noises,
with dark day-songs.
To whom can I leave so much,
so much and so little,
joy beyond its objects,
a lone horse by the sea,
a loom weaving the wind?

And hands on his joys

My own sorrows I leave to
all those who made me suffer
but by now I've forgotten them
and I don't know where I lost them —
if they turn up in the forest
they're like tangleweed.
They grow from the ground up
and end where you end,
at your head, at the air —
to keep them from growing,
spring has to be changed.

Se pronuncia en contra del odio

Anduve acercándome al odio,
son serios sus escalofríos,
sus nociones vertiginosas.
El odio es un pez espada,
se mueve en el agua invisible
y entonces se le ve venir,
y tiene sangre en el cuchillo:
lo desarma la transparencia.

Entonces para qué odiar
a los que tanto nos odiaron?
Allí están debajo del agua
acechadores y acostados
preparando espada y alcuza,
telarañas y telaperros
No se trata de cristianismos,
no es oración ni sastrería,
sino que el odio perdió:
se le cayeron las escamas
en el mercado del veneno,
y mientras tanto sale el sol
y uno se pone a trabajar
y a comprar su pan y su vino.

Pero lo considera en su testamento

Al odio le dejaré
mis herraduras de caballo,
mi camiseta de navío,
mis zapatos de caminante,

He comes out against hate

I've come within range of hate.
Terrifying, its tremors,
its dizzying obsessions.
Hate's like a swordfish
invisible in the water,
knifing suddenly into sight
with blood on its blade—
clear water misleads you.

Why, why do we hate so much
those who hate us?
There they are underwater,
hunters lying in wait,
swords and oilcans ready,
spiderwebs and mousetraps.
It has nothing to do with being Christian,
or with prayer or with tailoring;
it's just that hate is a loser.
Scales fell from eyes
in the poison market;
meanwhile the sun comes out
and I start to work
and to buy bread and wine.

But deals with it in his will

To hate I'll leave
my own horseshoes,
my sailor's shirt,
my traveler's shoes,

mi corazón de carpintero,
todo lo que supe hacer
y lo que me ayudó a sufrir,
lo que tuve de duro y puro,
de indisoluble y emigrante,
para que se aprenda en el mundo
que los que tienen bosque y agua
pueden cortar y navegar,
pueden ir y pueden volver,
pueden padecer y amar,
pueden temer y trabajar,
pueden ser y pueden seguir,
pueden florecer y morir,
pueden ser sencillos y oscuros,
pueden no tener orejas,
pueden aguantar la desdicha,
pueden esperar una flor,
en fin, podemos existir,
aunque no acepten nuestras vidas
unos cuantos hijos de puta.

Finalmente, se dirige con arrobamiento a su amada

Matilde Urrutia, aquí te dejo
lo que tuve y lo que no tuve,
lo que soy y lo que no soy.
Mi amor es un niño que llora,
no quiere salir de tus brazos,
yo te lo dejo para siempre:
eres para mí la más bella.

my carpenter's heart,
all things I did well,
and which helped me to suffer,
the strong clear things I had,
permanent and passing,
so that it dawns on the world
that those who have trees and water
can carve ships, set sail,
can go away and come back,
suffer and love,
have fears, do work,
be and go on being,
be fruitful and die,
be simple and complex,
not have ears,
turn misery to account,
wait for a flower's coming—
in a word, live;
although there are always some shitheads
who will not accept our lives.

At last he turns in ecstasy to his love

Matilde Urrutia, I'm leaving you here
all I had, all I didn't have,
all I am, all I am not.
My love is a child crying,
reluctant to leave your arms,
I leave it to you forever—
you are my chosen one.

Eres para mí la más bella,
la más tatuada por el viento,
como un arbolito del sur,
como un avellano en agosto,
eres para mí suculenta
como una panadería,
es de tierra tu corazón
pero tus manos son celestes.

Eres roja y eres picante,
eres blanca y eres salada
como escabeche de cebolla,
eres un piano que ríe
con todas las notas del alma
y sobre mí cae la música
de tus pestañas y tu pelo,
me baño en tu sombra de oro
y me deleitan tus orejas
como si las hubiera visto,
en las mareas de coral:
por tus uñas luché en las olas
contra pescados pavorosos.

De sur a sur se abren tus ojos,
y de este a oeste tu sonrisa,
no se te pueden ver los pies,
y el sol se entretiene estrellando
el amanecer en tu pelo.
Tu cuerpo y tu rostro llegaron
como yo, de regiones duras,
de ceremonias lluviosas,
de antiguas tierras y martirios,

You are my chosen one,
more tempered by winds
than thin trees in the south,
a hazel in August;
for me you are as delicious
as a great bakery.
You have an earth heart
but your hands are from heaven.

You are red and spicy,
you are white and salty
like pickled onions,
you are a laughing piano
with every human note;
and music runs over me
from your eyelashes and your hair.
I wallow in your gold shadow,
I'm enchanted by your ears
as though I had seen them before
in underwater coral.
In the sea for your nails' sake,
I took on terrifying fish.

Your eyes widen from south to south,
your smile goes east and west;
your feet can hardly be seen,
and the sun takes pleasure
in dawning in your hair.
Your face and your body come from
hard places, as I do,
from rain-washed rituals,
ancient lands and martyrs.

sigue cantando el Bío Bío
en nuestra arcilla ensangrentada,
pero tú trajiste del bosque
todos los secretos perfumes
y esa manera de lucir
un perfil de flecha perdida,
una medalla de guerrero.
Tú fuiste mi vencedora
por el amor y por la tierra,
porque tu boca me traía
antepasados manantiales,
citas en bosques de otra edad,
oscuros tambores mojados:
de pronto oí que me llamaban:
era de lejos y de cuando:
me acerqué al antiguo follaje
y besé mi sangre en tu boca,
corazón mío, mi araucana.

Qué puedo dejarte si tienes,
Matilde Urrutia, en tu contacto
ese aroma de hojas quemadas,
esa fragancia de frutillas
y entre tus dos pechos marinos
el crepúsculo de Cauquenes
y el olor de peumo de Chile?

En el alto otoño del mar
lleno de niebla y cavidades,
la tierra se extiende y respira,
se le caen al mes las hojas.

The Bío-Bío still sings
in our bloodstained clay,
but you brought from the forest
every secret scent,
and the way your profile has of shining
like a lost arrow,
an old warrior's medal.
You overcame me
with love and origins,
because your mouth brought back
ancient beginnings,
forest meetings from another time,
dark ancestral drums.
I suddenly heard myself summoned —
it was far away, vague.
I moved close to ancient foliage.
I touched my blood in your mouth,
dear love, my Araucana.

What can I leave you, Matilde,
when you have at your touch
that aura of burning leaves,
that fragrance of strawberries,
and between your sea-breasts
the half-light of Cauquenes,
and the laurel-smell of Chile?

It is high autumn at sea,
full of mists and hidden places;
the land stretches and breathes,
leaves fall by the month.

Y tú inclinada en mi trabajo
con tu pasión y tu paciencia
deletreando las patas verdes,
las telarañas, los insectos
de mi mortal caligrafía,
oh leona de pies pequeñitos,
qué haría sin tus manos breves?
dónde andaría caminando
sin corazón y sin objeto?
en qué lejanos autobuses,
enfermo de fuego o de nieve?

Te debo el otoño marino
con la humedad de las raíces,
y la niebla como una uva,
y el sol silvestre y elegante:
te debo este cajón callado
en que se pierden los dolores
y sólo suben a la frente
las corolas de la alegría.
Todo te lo debo a ti,
tórtola desencadenada,
mi codorniza copetona,
mi jilguero de las montañas,
mi campesina de Coihueco.

Alguna vez si ya no somos,
si ya no vamos ni venimos
bajo siete capas de polvo
y los pies secos de la muerte,

And you, bent over my work,
with both passion and patience,
deciphering the green prints,
the spiderwebs, the insects
of my fateful handwriting.
Lioness on your little feet,
what would I do without
the neat ways of your hands?
Where would I be wandering
with no heart, with no end?
On what faraway buses,
flushed with fire or snow?

I owe you marine autumn
with dankness at its roots
and fog like a grape
and the graceful sun of the country;
and the silent space
in which sorrows lose themselves
and only the bright crown
of joy comes to the surface.
I owe you it all,
my unchained dove,
my crested quail,
my mountain finch,
my peasant from Coihueco.

Sometime when we've stopped being,
stopped coming and going,
under seven blankets of dust
and the dry feet of death,

estaremos juntos, amor,
extrañamente confundidos.
Nuestras espinas diferentes,
nuestros ojos maleducados,
nuestros pies que no se encontraban
y nuestros besos indelebles,
todo estará por fin reunido,
pero de qué nos servirá
la unidad en un cementerio?
Que no nos separe la vida
y se vaya al diablo la muerte!

Recomendaciones finales

Aquí me despido, señores,
después de tantas despedidas
y como no les dejo nada
quiero que todos toquen algo:
lo más inclemente que tuve,
lo más insano y más ferviente
vuelve a la tierra y vuelve a ser:
los pétalos de la bondad
cayeron como campanadas
en la boca verde del viento.

Pero yo recogí con creces
la bondad de amigos y ajenos.
Me recibía la bondad
por donde pasé caminando
y la encontré por todas partes
como un corazón repartido.

we'll be close again, love,
curious and puzzled.
Our different feathers,
our bumbling eyes,
our feet which didn't meet
and our printed kisses,
all will be back together,
but what good will it do us,
the closeness of a grave?
Let life not separate us;
and who cares about death?

Last remarks

So I'm saying goodbye, gentlemen,
after so many farewells;
and since I'm leaving nothing,
I want everyone to have something;
the stormiest thing I had,
the craziest and most seething
comes back to earth, comes back to life.
The petals of well-wishing
fell like bells
in the green mouth of the wind.

But I've had in abundance
the bounty of friends and strangers.
I've found generosity
wherever my ways took me
and I found it everywhere
like a shared-out heart.

Qué fronteras medicinales
no destronaron mi destierro
compartiendo conmigo el pan,
el peligro, el techo y el vino?
El mundo abrió sus arboledas
y entré como Juan por su casa
entre dos filas de ternura.
Tengo en el Sur tantos amigos
como los que tengo en el Norte,
no se puede poner el sol
entre mis amigos del Este,
y cuántos son en el Oeste?
No puedo numerar el trigo.
No puedo nombrar ni contar
los Oyarzunes fraternales:
en América sacudida
por tanta amenaza nocturna
no hay luna que no me conozca
ni caminos que no me esperen:
en los pobres pueblos de arcilla
o en las ciudades de cemento
hay algún Arce remoto
que no conozco todavía
pero que nacimos hermanos.

En todas partes recogí
la miel que devoran los osos,
la sumergida primavera,
el tesoro del elefante,
y eso se lo debo a los míos,
a mis parientes cristalinos.

Nor did medicinal frontiers
ever upset my exile—
they shared bread with me,
danger, shelter, wine.
The world threw open its orchards
and I went in, like Jack to his house,
between two rows of tenderness.
I have as many friends in the South
as I have in the North,
the sun could never set
on my friends in the East—
and how many in the West?
I can't count the wheat.
I can't number or count
my friends among the Oyarzunes.
In America, shaken by
so much night-fear,
there's not a moon doesn't know me,
no roads that don't expect me,
in the poor clay villages
or the concrete cities
there's some remote Arce
whom I don't know yet
except we were born brothers.

Everywhere I gathered
the honey that bears devour,
the secret stirrings of spring,
the treasure of the elephants,
and that I leave to my own ones,
the clear stream of my family.

El pueblo me identificó
y nunca dejé de ser pueblo.
Tuve en la palma de la mano
el mundo con sus archipiélagos
y como soy irrenunciable
no renuncié a mi corazón,
a las ostras ni a las estrellas.

*Termina su libro el poeta hablando de sus variadas transformaciones y
confirmando su fe en la poesía*

De tantas veces que he nacido
tengo una experiencia salobre
como criatura del mar
con celestiales atavismos
y con destinación terrestre.
Y así me muevo sin saber
a qué mundo voy a volver
o si voy a seguir viviendo.
Mientras se resuelven las cosas
aquí dejé mi testimonio,
mi navegante estravagario
para que leyéndolo mucho
nadie pudiera aprender nada,
sino el movimiento perpetuo
de un hombre claro y confundido,
de un hombre lluvioso y alegre,
enérgico y otoñabundo.

Y ahora detrás de esta hoja
me voy y no desaparezco:

The people defined me
and I never stopped being one of them.
I held in the palm of my hand
the world with its archipelagoes
and since I can't be denied,
I never denied my heart,
or oysters, or stars.

*The poet ends his book by talking about his transformations and
confirms his faith in poetry*

From having been born so often
I have salty experience
like creatures of the sea
with a passion for stars
and an earthy destination.
And so I move without knowing
to which world I'll be returning
or if I'll go on living.
While things are settling down,
here I've left my testament,
my shifting extravagaria,
so whoever goes on reading it
will never take in anything
except the constant moving
of a clear and bewildered man,
a man rainy and happy,
lively and autumn-minded.

And now I'm going behind
this page, but not disappearing.

daré un salto en la transparencia
como un nadador del cielo,
y luego volveré a crecer
hasta ser tan pequeño un día
que el viento me llevará
y no sabré cómo me llamo
y no seré cuando despierte:

entonces cantaré en silencio.

I'll dive into clear air
like a swimmer in the sky,
and then get back to growing
till one day I'm so small
that the wind will take me away
and I won't know my own name
and I won't be there when I wake.

Then I will sing in the silence.

ALASTAIR REID

FROM

Navegaciones
y regresos

Navigations
and Returns

(1957–59)

ODA AL ELEFANTE

Espesa bestia pura,
San Elefante,
animal santo
del bosque sempiterno,
todo materia fuerte,
fina
y equilibrada,
cuero
de
talabartería planetaria,
marfil
compacto, satinado,
sereno
como
la carne de la luna,
ojos mínimos
para mirar, no para ser mirados,
y trompa
tocadora,
corneta
del contacto,
manguera
del
animal
gozoso
en
su
frescura,

ODE TO THE ELEPHANT

Thick, pristine beast,
Saint Elephant,
sacred animal
of perennial forests,
sheer strength,
fine
and balanced
leather
of
global saddle-makers,
compact,
satin-finished ivory,
serene
like
the moon's flesh,
with minuscule eyes
to see—and not be seen—
and a singing trunk,
a blowing horn,
hose
of
the
creature
rejoicing
in
its
own
freshness,

máquina movediza,
teléfono del bosque,
y así
pasa tranquilo
y bamboleante
con su vieja envoltura,
con su ropaje
de árbol arrugado,
su pantalón
caído
y su colita.

No nos equivoquemos.
La dulce y grande bestia de la selva
no es el *clown*,
sino el padre,
el padre en la luz verde,
es el antiguo
y puro
progenitor terrestre.

Total fecundación,
tantálica
codicia,
fornicación
y piel
mayoritaria,
costumbres
en la lluvia
rodearon
el reino
de los elefantes,

shaking machine
and forest telephone,
this is how
the elephant passes by,
tranquil,
parading his ancient façade,
his costume
made of
wrinkled trees,
his pants
falling down,
and his teeny tail.

Make no mistake:
this gentle, huge jungle beast
is not a clown
but a father,
a priest of green light,
an earthly progenitor,
ancient
and whole.

Bountiful
in its tantalizing
avarice,
made of skin
and fornication,
the elephant kingdom
grew
accustomed
to the rain.

y fue
con sal
y sangre
la genérica guerra
en el silencio.

Las escamosas formas,
el lagarto león,
el pez montaña,
el milodonto cíclope,
cayeron,
decayeron,
fueron fermento verde en el pantano,
tesoro
de las tórridas moscas,
de escarabajos crueles.
Emergió el elefante
del miedo destronado.
Fue casi vegetal, oscura torre
del firmamento verde,
y de hojas dulces, miel
y agua de roca
se alimentó su estirpe.

Iba pues por la selva
el elefante con su paz profunda.

But then came
a universal war,
bringing
silence
with salt and blood.

The scaly forms
of lizard-lion,
mountain-fish,
magisterial Cyclops
fell away,
decayed,
fresh ferment on the marsh,
a treasure
for torrid flies
and cruel beetles.
The elephant awakened
from its dethroned fear,
but almost vegetative,
a dark tower
in the olive firmament, his lineage
nurtured by sweet leaves,
honey
and rock water.

Thus he wandered through the forest,
in weighty peace,

Iba condecorado
por
las órdenes más claras
del rocío,
sensible
a la
humedad
de su universo,
enorme, triste y tierno
hasta que lo encontraron
y lo hicieron
bestia de circo envuelta
por el olor humano,
sin aire para su intranquila trompa,
sin tierra para sus terrestres patas.
Lo vi entrar aquel día,
y lo recuerdo como a un moribundo,
lo vi entrar al Kraal, al perseguido.
Fue en Ceylán, en la selva.
Los tambores,
el fuego,
habían desviado
su ruta de rocío,
y allí fue rodeado.
Entre el aullido y el silencio entró
como un inmenso rey. No comprendía.
Su reino era una cárcel, sin embargo
era el sol como siempre, palpitaba
la luz libre, seguía verde el mundo,
con lentitud tocó la empalizada,
no las lanzas, y a mí,
a mí entre todos,

sensitive to the humidity of the universe,
decorated
with
the clearest commands
of the dew,
enormous,
sad and tender,
until they found him
and turned him
into a circus beast,
wrapped in human smells,
unable to breathe
through his restless trunk,
without earth
 for his earthly feet.
I saw him coming in that day.
I remember his agony.
I saw the damned creature entering the Kraal,
in the jungle of Ceylon.
Drums and fire
had changed his path of dew,
and he was surrounded.
Like an immense king
he arrived,
caught between howl and silence.
He understood nothing.
His kingdom was a prison,
yet the sun was still the sun,
palpitating free light,
and the world was still verdant.
Slowly, the elephant touched the stockade
and chose me from everyone else.

no sé, tal vez no pudo ser, no ha sido,
pero a mí me miró
con sus ojos secretos
y aún me duelen
los ojos
de aquel encarcelado,
de aquel inmenso rey preso en su selva.

Por eso hoy rememoro tu mirada,
elefante perdido
entre las duras lanzas
y las hojas
y en tu honor, bestia pura,
levanto los collares
de mi oda
para que te pasees
por el mundo
con mi infiel poesía
que entonces no podía defenderte,
pero que ahora
junta
en el recuerdo
la empalizada en donde aprisionaron
el honor animal de tu estatura
y aquellos dulces ojos de elefante
que allí perdieron todo lo que habían amado.

I don't know why. Maybe it wasn't so,
could not have been,
but he looked at me
between the stakes
with his secret eyes.
His eyes
still pain me,
a prisoner's eyes,
the immense king captive in his own jungle.

That's why I invoke your gaze today,
elephant,
lost between the hard stakes
and the leaves.
In your honor, pristine beast,
I lift the collar
of my ode
so you may walk through the world again.
My unfaithful poetry
was unable to defend you then.
Now I bring you back
through memory,
along with the stockade caging
your animal honor,
measured only by your height,
and those gentle eyes,
deprived forever of all they had once loved.

ILAN STAVANS

ODA A LA SANDÍA

El árbol del verano
intenso,
invulnerable,
es todo cielo azul,
sol amarillo,
cansancio a goterones,
es una espada
sobre los caminos,
un zapato quemado
en las ciudades:
la claridad, el mundo
nos agobian,
nos pegan
en los ojos
con polvareda,
con súbitos golpes de oro,
nos acosan
los pies
con espinitas,
con piedras calurosas,
y la boca
sufre
más que todos los dedos:
tienen sed
la garganta,
la dentadura,
los labios y la lengua:
queremos
beber las cataratas,

ODE TO THE WATERMELON

The tree of summer,
intense,
invulnerable,
is all blue sky,
yellow sun,
exhaustion dripping.
It's a sword above the roads,
a burnt shoe
in the cities:
clarity and the world
overwhelm us,
hit us
in the eye
with dust,
with sudden blows of gold;
they harass
our feet
with thorns,
with heated stones,
and the mouth
suffers
more than all the toes:
the throat
is thirsty,
the teeth,
the lips and tongue:
we want
to drink waterfalls,

la noche azul,
el polo,
y entonces
cruza el cielo
el más fresco de todos
los planetas,
la redonda, suprema
y celestial sandía.

Es la fruta del árbol de la sed.
Es la ballena verde del verano.

El universo seco
de pronto
tachonado
por este firmamento de frescura
deja caer
la fruta
rebosante:
se abren sus hemisferios
mostrando una bandera
verde, blanca, escarlata,
que se disuelve
en cascada, en azúcar,
en delicia!

Cofre del agua, plácida
reina
de la frutería,
bodega
de la profundidad, luna
terrestre!

the blue night,
the pole.
Just then
the coolest of all planets
crosses the sky,
the rounded, supreme
and celestial watermelon.

It's the fruit from the tree of thirst.
It's the green whale of summer.

The dry universe,
suddenly
marked
by this firmament of
coolness,
allows
the fruit
to drop:
its hemispheres open,
showing a flag
—green, white, scarlet—
dissolving itself
in cascades, sugar,
delight!

Water coffer,
placid fruit
queen,
warehouse
of depth,
earthly moon!

Oh pura,
en tu abundancia
se deshacen rubíes
y uno
quisiera
morderte
hundiendo
en ti
la cara,
el pelo,
el alma!
Te divisamos
en la sed
como
mina o montaña
de espléndido alimento,
pero
te conviertes
entre la dentadura y el deseo
en sólo
fresca luz
que se deslíe,
en manantial
que nos tocó
cantando.
Y así
no pesas
en la siesta
abrasadora,
no pesas,
sólo
pasas

Oh, purity
incarnate,
rubies fall apart
in your abundance.
We would like
to bite you,
sinking
the face,
the hair,
the soul
into you!
Thirsty,
we see you
like
a mine or mountain
of splendid food,
but
you transform
between our teeth and desire
into
fresh light that unleashes us,
becoming
a spring
that touches us,
singing.
And then,
you're
weightless
in the all-embracing
siesta,
only
passing by,

y tu gran corazón de brasa fría
se convirtió en el agua
de una gota.

and your great heart of cold coal
is transformed into water
contained in a single drop.

ILAN STAVANS

FROM

Cien
sonetos de amor

One Hundred
Love Sonnets

(1957–59)

IV

Recordarás aquella quebrada caprichosa
a donde los aromas palpitantes treparon,
de cuando en cuando un pájaro vestido
con agua y lentitud: traje de invierno.

Recordarás los dones de la tierra:
irascible fragancia, barro de oro,
hierbas del matorral, locas raíces,
sortílegas espinas como espadas.

Recordarás el ramo que trajiste,
ramo de sombra y agua con silencio,
ramo como una piedra con espuma.

Y aquella vez fue como nunca y siempre:
vamos allí donde no espera nada
y hallamos todo lo que está esperando.

IV

You will remember that leaping stream
where sweet aromas rose and trembled,
and sometimes a bird, wearing water
and slowness, its winter feathers.

You will remember those gifts from the earth:
indelible scents, gold clay,
weeds in the thicket and crazy roots,
magical thorns like swords.

You'll remember the bouquet you picked,
shadows and silent water,
bouquet like a foam-covered stone.

That time was like never, and like always.
So we go there, where nothing is waiting;
we find everything waiting there.

STEPHEN TAPSCOTT

XI

Tengo hambre de tu boca, de tu voz, de tu pelo
y por las calles voy sin nutrirme, callado,
no me sostiene el pan, el alba me desquicia,
busco el sonido líquido de tus pies en el día.

Estoy hambriento de tu risa resbalada,
de tus manos color de furioso granero,
tengo hambre de la pálida piedra de tus uñas,
quiero comer tu piel como una intacta almendra.

Quiero comer el rayo quemado en tu hermosura,
la nariz soberana del arrogante rostro,
quiero comer la sombra fugaz de tus pestañas

y hambriento vengo y voy olfateando el crepúsculo
buscándote, buscando tu corazón caliente
como un puma en la soledad de Quitratúe.

I crave your mouth, your voice, your hair.
Silent and starving, I prowl through the streets.
Bread does not nourish me, dawn disrupts me, all day
I hunt for the liquid measure of your steps.

I hunger for your sleek laugh,
your hands the color of a savage harvest,
hunger for the pale stones of your fingernails,
I want to eat your skin like a whole almond.

I want to eat the sunbeam flaring in your lovely body,
the sovereign nose of your arrogant face,
I want to eat the fleeting shade of your lashes,

and I pace around hungry, sniffing the twilight,
hunting for you, for your hot heart,
like a puma in the barrens of Quitratúe.

STEPHEN TAPSCOTT

XVI

Amo el trozo de tierra que tú eres,
porque de las praderas planetarias
otra estrella no tengo. Tú repites
la multiplicación del universo.

Tus anchos ojos son la luz que tengo
de las constelaciones derrotadas,
tu piel palpita como los caminos
que recorre en la lluvia el meteoro.

De tanta luna fueron para mí tus caderas,
de todo el sol tu boca profunda y su delicia
de tanta luz ardiente como miel en la sombra

tu corazón quemado por largos rayos rojos,
y así recorro el fuego de tu forma besándote,
pequeña y planetaria, paloma y geografía.

XVI

I love the handful of the earth you are.
Because of its meadows, vast as a planet,
I have no other star. You are my replica
of the multiplying universe.

Your wide eyes are the only light I know
from extinguished constellations;
your skin throbs like the streak
of a meteor through rain.

Your hips were that much of the moon for me;
your deep mouth and its delights, that much sun;
your heart, fiery with its long red rays,

was that much ardent light, like honey in the shade.
So I pass across your burning form, kissing
you — compact and planetary, my dove, my globe.

STEPHEN TAPSCOTT

XLVIII

Dos amantes dichosos hacen un solo pan,
una sola gota de luna en la hierba,
dejan andando dos sombras que se reúnen,
dejan un solo sol vacío en una cama.

De todas las verdades escogieron el día:
no se ataron con hilos sino con un aroma,
y no despedazaron la paz ni las palabras.
La dicha es una torre transparente.

El aire, el vino van con los dos amantes,
la noche les regala sus pétalos dichosos,
tienen derecho a todos los claveles.

Dos amantes dichosos no tienen fin ni muerte,
nacen y mueren muchas veces mientras viven,
tienen la eternidad de la naturaleza.

XLVIII

Two happy lovers make one bread,
a single moon drop in the grass.
Walking, they cast two shadows that flow together;
waking, they leave one sun empty in their bed.

Of all the possible truths, they chose the day;
they held it, not with ropes but with an aroma.
They did not shred the peace; they did not shatter words;
their happiness is a transparent tower.

The air and wine accompany the lovers.
The night delights them with its joyous petals.
They have a right to all the carnations.

Two happy lovers, without an ending, with no death,
they are born, they die, many times while they live:
they have the eternal life of the Natural.

STEPHEN TAPSCOTT

LXXX

De viajes y dolores yo regresé, amor mío,
a tu voz, a tu mano volando en la guitarra,
al fuego que interrumpe con besos el otoño,
a la circulación de la noche en el cielo.

Para todos los hombres pido pan y reinado,
pido tierra para el labrador sin ventura,
que nadie espere tregua de mi sangre o mi canto.
Pero a tu amor no puedo renunciar sin morirme.

Por eso toca el vals de la serena luna,
la barcarola en el agua de la guitarra
hasta que se doblegue mi cabeza soñando:

que todos los desvelos de mi vida tejieron
esta enramada en donde tu mano vive y vuela
custodiando la noche del viajero dormido.

LXXX

My love, I returned from travel and sorrow
to your voice, to your hand flying on the guitar,
to the fire interrupting the autumn with kisses,
to the night that circles through the sky.

I ask for bread and dominion for all;
for the worker with no future I ask for land.
May no one expect my blood or my song to rest!
But I cannot give up your love, not without dying.

So: play the waltz of the tranquil moon,
the barcarole, on the fluid guitar,
till my head lolls, dreaming:

for all my life's sleeplessness has woven
this shelter in the grove where your hand lives and flies,
watching over the night of the sleeping traveler.

STEPHEN TAPSCOTT

XC

Pensé morir, sentí de cerca el frío,
y de cuanto viví sólo a ti te dejaba:
tu boca eran mi día y mi noche terrestres
y tu piel la república fundada por mis besos.

En ese instante se terminaron los libros,
la amistad, los tesoros sin tregua acumulados,
la casa transparente que tú y yo construimos:
todo dejó de ser, menos tus ojos.

Porque el amor, mientras la vida nos acosa,
es simplemente una ola alta sobre las olas
pero ay cuando la muerte viene a tocar la puerta

hay sólo tu mirada para tanto vacío,
sólo tu claridad para no seguir siendo,
sólo tu amor para cerrar la sombra.

I thought I was dying, I felt the cold up close
and knew that from all my life I left only you behind:
my earthly day and night were your mouth,
your skin the republic my kisses founded.

In that instant the books stopped,
and friendship, treasures restlessly amassed,
the transparent house that you and I built:
everything dropped away, except your eyes.

Because while life harasses us, love is
only a wave taller than the other waves:
but oh, when death comes knocking at the gate,

there is only your glance against so much emptiness,
only your light against extinction,
only your love to shut out the shadows.

STEPHEN TAPSCOTT

XCVII

Hay que volar en este tiempo, a dónde?
Sin alas, sin avión, volar sin duda:
ya los pasos pasaron sin remedio,
no elevaron los pies del pasajero.

Hay que volar a cada instante como
las águilas, las moscas y los días,
hay que vencer los ojos de Saturno
y establecer allí nuevas campanas.

Ya no bastan zapatos ni caminos,
ya no sirve la tierra a los errantes,
ya cruzaron la noche las raíces,

y tú aparecerás en otra estrella
determinadamente transitoria
convertida por fin en amapola.

XCVII

These days, one must fly—but where to?
without wings, without an airplane, fly—without a doubt:
the footsteps have passed on, to no avail;
they didn't move the feet of the traveler along.

At every instant, one must fly—like
eagles, like houseflies, like days:
must conquer the rings of Saturn
and build new carillons there.

Shoes and pathways are no longer enough,
the earth is no use anymore to the wanderer:
the roots have already crossed through the night,

and you will appear on another planet,
stubbornly transient,
transformed in the end into poppies.

STEPHEN TAPSCOTT

Plenos poderes

✳

Fully Empowered

(1961–62)

DEBER DEL POETA

A quien no escucha el mar en este viernes
por la mañana, quien adentro de algo,
casa, oficina, fábrica o mujer,
o calle o mina o seco calabozo:
a éste yo acudo y sin hablar ni ver
llego y abro la puerta del encierro
y un sin fin se oye vago en la insistencia,
un largo trueno roto se encadena
al peso del planeta y de la espuma,
surgen los ríos roncos del océno,
vibra veloz en su rosal la estrella
y el mar palpita, muere y continúa.

Así por el destino conducido
debo sin tregua oír y conservar
el lamento marino en mi conciencia,
debo sentir el golpe de agua dura
y recogerlo en una taza eterna
para que donde esté el encarcelado,
donde sufra el castigo del otoño
yo esté presente con una ola errante,
yo circule a través de las ventanas
y al oírme levante la mirada
diciendo: cómo me acercaré al océano?
Y yo transmitiré sin decir nada
los ecos estrellados de la ola,
un quebranto de espuma y arenales,
un susurro de sal que se retira,
el grito gris del ave de la costa.

THE POET'S OBLIGATION

To whoever is not listening to the sea
this Friday morning, to whoever is cooped up
in house or office, factory or woman
or street or mine or dry prison cell,
to him I come, and without speaking or looking
I arrive and open the door of his prison,
and a vibration starts up, vague and insistent,
a long rumble of thunder adds itself
to the weight of the planet and the foam,
the groaning rivers of the ocean rise,
the star vibrates quickly in its corona
and the sea beats, dies, and goes on beating.

So, drawn on by my destiny,
I ceaselessly must listen to and keep
the sea's lamenting in my consciousness,
I must feel the crash of the hard water
and gather it up in a perpetual cup
so that, wherever those in prison may be,
wherever they suffer the sentence of the autumn,
I may be present with an errant wave,
I may move in and out of windows,
and hearing me, eyes may lift themselves,
asking "How can I reach the sea?"
And I will pass to them, saying nothing,
the starry echoes of the wave,
a breaking up of foam and quicksand,
a rustling of salt withdrawing itself,
the gray cry of sea birds on the coast.

Y así, por mí, la libertad y el mar
responderán al corazón oscuro.

So, through me, freedom and the sea
will call in answer to the shrouded heart.

ALASTAIR REID

LA PALABRA

Nació
la palabra en la sangre,
creció en el cuerpo oscuro, palpitando,
y voló con los labios y la boca.

Más lejos y más cerca
aún, aún venía
de padres muertos y de errantes razas,
de territorios que se hicieron piedra,
que se cansaron de sus pobres tribus,
porque cuando el dolor salió al camino
los pueblos anduvieron y llegaron
y nueva tierra y agua reunieron
para sembrar de nuevo su palabra.
Y así la herencia es ésta:
éste es el aire que nos comunica
con el hombre enterrado y con la aurora
de nuevos seres que aún no amanecieron.

Aún la atmósfera tiembla
con la primera palabra
elaborada
con pánico y gemido.
Salió
de las tinieblas
y hasta ahora no hay trueno
que truene aún con su ferretería
como aquella palabra,

THE WORD

The word
was born in the blood,
grew in the dark body, beating,
and took flight through the lips and the mouth.

Farther away and nearer
still, still it came
from dead fathers and from wandering races,
from lands which had turned to stone,
lands weary of their poor tribes,
for when grief took to the roads
the people set out and arrived
and married new land and water
to grow their words again.
And so this is the inheritance;
this is the wavelength which connects us
with dead men and the dawning
of new beings not yet come to light.

Still the atmosphere quivers
with the first word uttered
dressed up
in terror and sighing.
It emerged
from the darkness
and until now there is no thunder
that ever rumbles with the iron voice
of that word,

la primera
palabra pronunciada:
tal vez sólo un susurro fue, una gota,
y cae y cae aún su catarata.

Luego el sentido llena la palabra.
Quedó preñada y se llenó de vidas.
Todo fue nacimientos y sonidos:
la afirmación, la claridad, la fuerza,
la negación, la destrucción, la muerte:
el verbo asumió todos los poderes
y se fundió existencia con esencia
en la electricidad de su hermosura.

Palabra humana, sílaba, cadera
de larga luz y dura platería,
hereditaria copa que recibe
las comunicaciones de la sangre:
he aquí que el silencio fue integrado
por el total de la palabra humana
y no hablar es morir entre los seres:
se hace lenguaje hasta la cabellera,
habla la boca sin mover los labios:
los ojos de repente son palabras.

Yo tomo la palabra y la recorro
como si fuera sólo forma humana,
me embelesan sus líneas y navego
en cada resonancia del idioma:
pronuncio y soy y sin hablar me acerca
el fin de las palabras al silencio.

the first
word uttered—
perhaps it was only a ripple, a single drop,
and yet its great cataract falls and falls.

Later on, the word fills with meaning.
Always with child, it filled up with lives.
Everything was births and sounds—
affirmation, clarity, strength,
negation, destruction, death—
the verb took over all the power
and blended existence with essence
in the electricity of its grace.

Human word, syllable, flank
of extending light and solid silverwork,
hereditary goblet which receives
the communications of the blood—
here is where silence came together with
the wholeness of the human word,
and, for human beings, not to speak is to die—
language extends even to the hair,
the mouth speaks without the lips moving,
all of a sudden, the eyes are words.

I take the word and pass it through my senses
as though it were no more than a human shape;
its arrangements awe me and I find my way
through each resonance of the spoken word—
I utter and I am and, speechless, I approach
across the edge of words silence itself.

Bebo por la palabra levantando
una palabra o copa cristalina,
en ella bebo
el vino del idioma
o el agua interminable,
manantial maternal de las palabras,
y copa y agua y vino
originan mi canto
porque el verbo es origen
y vierte vida: es sangre,
es la sangre que expresa su substancia
y está dispuesto así su desarrollo:
dan cristal al cristal, sangre a la sangre,
y dan vida a la vida las palabras.

I drink to the word, raising
a word or a shining cup;
in it I drink
the pure wine of language
or inexhaustible water,
maternal source of words,
and cup and water and wine
give rise to my song
because the verb is the source
and vivid life—it is blood,
blood which expresses its substance
and so ordains its own unwinding.
Words give glass quality to glass, blood to blood,
and life to life itself.

ALASTAIR REID

ADIOSES

Oh adioses a una tierra y otra tierra,
a cada boca y a cada tristeza,
a la luna insolente, a las semanas
que enrollaron los días y desaparecieron,
adiós a esta y aquella voz teñida
de amaranto, y adiós
a la cama y al plato de costumbre,
al sitio vesperal de los adioses,
a la silla casada con el mismo crepúsculo,
al camino que hicieron mis zapatos.

Me difundí, no hay duda,
me cambié de existencias,
cambié de piel, de lámpara, de odios,
tuve que hacerlo
no por ley ni capricho,
sino que por cadena,
me encadenó cada nuevo camino,
le tomé gusto a tierra a toda tierra.

Y pronto dije adiós, recién llegado,
con la ternura aún recién partida
como si el pan se abriera y de repente
huyera todo el mundo de la mesa.
Así me fui de todos los idiomas,
repetí los adioses como una puerta vieja,
cambié de cine, de razón, de tumba,
me fui de todas partes a otra parte,
seguí siendo y siguiendo

GOODBYES

Goodbye, goodbye, to one place or another,
to every mouth, to every sorrow,
to the insolent moon, to weeks
which wound in the days and disappeared,
goodbye to this voice and that one stained
with amaranth, and goodbye
to the usual bed and plate,
to the twilit setting of all goodbyes,
to the chair that is part of the same twilight,
to the way made by my shoes.

I spread myself, no question;
I turned over whole lives,
changed skin, lamps, and hates,
it was something I had to do,
not by law or whim,
more of a chain reaction;
each new journey enchained me;
I took pleasure in place, in all places.

And, newly arrived, I promptly said goodbye
with still newborn tenderness
as if the bread were to open and suddenly
flee from the world of the table.
So I left behind all languages,
repeated goodbyes like an old door,
changed cinemas, reasons, and tombs,
left everywhere for somewhere else;
I went on being, and being always

medio desmantelado en la alegría,
nupcial en la tristeza,
sin saber nunca cómo ni cuándo,
listo para volver, mas no se vuelve.

Se sabe que el que vuelve no se fue,
y así la vida anduve y desanduve
mudándome de traje y de planeta,
acostumbrándome a la compañía,
a la gran muchedumbre del destierro,
a la gran soledad de las campanas.

half undone with joy,
a bridegroom among sadnesses,
never knowing how or when,
ready to return, never returning.

It's well known that he who returns never left,
so I traced and retraced my life,
changing clothes and planets,
growing used to the company,
to the great whirl of exile,
to the great solitude of bells tolling.

ALASTAIR REID

PASADO

Tenemos que echar abajo el pasado
y como se construye
piso por piso, ventana a ventana,
y sube el edificio
así, bajando vamos
primero tejas rotas,
luego orgullosas puertas,
hasta que del pasado
sale polvo
como si se golpeara
contra el suelo,
sale humo
como si se quemara,
y cada nuevo día
reluce
como un plato
vacío:
no hay nada, no hubo nada:
hay que llenarlo
de nuevas nutriciones
espaciosas,
entonces, hacia abajo
cae el día de ayer
como en un pozo
al agua del pasado,
a la cisterna
de lo que ya no tiene voz ni fuego.
Es difícil
acostumbrar los huesos

PAST

We have to discard the past
and, as one builds
floor by floor, window by window,
and the building rises,
so do we keep shedding—
first, broken tiles,
then proud doors,
until, from the past,
dust falls
as if it would crash
against the floor,
smoke rises
as if it were on fire,
and each new day
gleams
like an empty
plate.
There is nothing, there was always nothing.
It all has to be filled
with a new, expanding
fruitfulness;
then, down
falls yesterday
as in a well
falls yesterday's water,
into the cistern
of all that is now without voice, without fire.
It is difficult
to get bones used

a perderse,
los ojos
a cerrarse
pero
lo hacemos
sin saberlo:
todo era vivo,
vivo, vivo, vivo
como un pez escarlata
pero el tiempo
pasó con trapo y noche
y fue borrando
el pez y su latido:
al agua al agua al agua
va cayendo el pasado
aunque se agarre
a espinas
y raíces:
se fue se fue y no valen
los recuerdos:
ya el párpado sombrío
cubrió la luz del ojo
y aquello que vivía
ya no vive:
lo que fuimos no somos.
Y la palabra aunque las letras tengan
iguales transparencias y vocales
ahora es otra y es otra la boca:
la misma boca es otra boca ahora:
cambiaron labios, piel, circulaciones,
otro ser ocupó nuestro esqueleto:
aquel que fue en nosotros ya no está:

to disappearing,
to teach eyes
to close,
but
we do it
unwittingly.
Everything was alive,
alive, alive, alive
like a scarlet fish,
but time
passed with cloth and darkness
and kept wiping away
the flash of the fish.
Water water water,
the past goes on falling
although it keeps a grip
on thorns
and on roots.
It went, it went, and now
memories mean nothing.
Now the heavy eyelid
shut out the light of the eye
and what was once alive
is now no longer living;
what we were, we are not.
And with words, although the letters
still have transparency and sound,
they change, and the mouth changes;
the same mouth is now another mouth;
they change, lips, skin, circulation;
another soul took on our skeleton;
what once was in us now is not.

se fue, pero si llaman, respondemos
"Aquí estoy" y se sabe que no estamos,
que aquel que estaba, estuvo y se perdió:
se perdió en el pasado y ya no vuelve.

It left, but if they call, we reply
"I am here," and we realize we are not,
that what was once, was and is lost,
lost in the past, and now does not come back.

ALASTAIR REID

EL PUEBLO

De aquel hombre me acuerdo y no han pasado
sino dos siglos desde que lo vi,
no anduvo ni a caballo ni en carroza:
a puro pie
deshizo
las distancias
y no llevaba espada ni armadura,
sino redes al hombro,
hacha o martillo o pala,
nunca apaleó a ninguno de su especie:
su hazaña fue contra el agua o la tierra,
contra el trigo para que hubiera pan,
contra el árbol gigante para que diera leña,
contra los muros para abrir las puertas,
contra la arena construyendo muros
y contra el mar para hacerlo parir.

Lo conocí y aún no se me borra.

Cayeron en pedazos las carrozas,
la guerra destruyó puertas y muros,
la ciudad fue un puñado de cenizas,
se hicieron polvo todos los vestidos,
y él para mí subsiste,
sobrevive en la arena,
cuando antes parecía
todo imborrable menos él.

That man I remember well, and at least two centuries
have passed since I last saw him;
he traveled neither on horseback nor in a carriage,
always on foot
he undid
the distances,
carrying neither sword nor weapon
but nets on his shoulder,
ax or hammer or spade;
he never fought with another of his kind—
his struggle was with water or with earth,
with the wheat, for it to become bread,
with the towering tree, for it to yield wood,
with walls, to open doors in them,
with sand, to form it into walls,
and with the sea, to make it bear fruit.

I knew him and he goes on haunting me.

The carriages splintered into pieces,
war destroyed doorways and walls,
the city was a fistful of ashes,
all the dresses shivered into dust,
and for me he persists,
he survives in the sand,
when everything previously
seemed durable except him.

En el ir y venir de las familias
a veces fue mi padre o mi pariente
o apenas si era él o si no era
tal vez aquel que no volvió a su casa
porque el agua o la tierra lo tragaron
o lo mató una máquina o un árbol
o fue aquel enlutado carpintero
que iba detrás del ataúd, sin lágrimas,
alguien en fin que no tenía nombre,
que se llamaba metal o madera,
y a quien miraron otros desde arriba
sin ver la hormiga
sino el hormiguero
y que cuando sus pies no se movían,
porque el pobre cansado había muerto,
no vieron nunca que no lo veían:
había ya otros pies en donde estuvo.

Los otros pies eran él mismo,
también las otras manos,
el hombre sucedía;
cuando ya parecía transcurrido
era el mismo de nuevo,
allí estaba otra vez cavando tierra,
cortando tela, pero sin camisa,
allí estaba y no estaba, como entonces,
se había ido y estaba de nuevo,
y como nunca tuvo cementerio,
ni tumba, ni su nombre fue grabado
sobre la piedra que cortó sudando,
nunca sabía nadie que llegaba
y nadie supo cuando se moría,

In the comings and goings of families,
sometimes he was my father or my relative
or almost was, or, if not, perhaps
the other one who never came back home
because water or earth swallowed him,
a machine or a tree killed him,
or he was that funeral carpenter
who walked behind the coffin, dry-eyed,
someone who never had a name
except as wood or metal have names,
and on whom others looked from above,
not noticing the ant,
only the anthill;
so that when his feet no longer moved
because, poor and tired, he had died,
they never saw what they were not used to seeing—
already other feet walked in his footsteps.

The other feet were still him,
the other hands as well.
The man persisted.
When it seemed he must be spent,
he was the same man over again;
there he was once more, digging the ground,
cutting cloth, but without a shirt,
he was there and he wasn't, just as before
he had gone away and replaced himself;
and since he never had cemetery
or tomb, or his name engraved
on the stone that he sweated to cut,
nobody ever knew of his arrival
and nobody knew when he died,

así es que sólo cuando el pobre pudo
resucitó otra vez sin ser notado.

Era el hombre sin duda, sin herencía,
sin vaca, sin bandera,
y no se distinguía entre los otros,
los otros que eran él,
desde arriba era gris como el subsuelo,
como el cuero era pardo,
era amarillo cosechando trigo,
era negro debajo de la mina,
era color de piedra en el castillo,
en el barco pesquero era color de atún
y color de caballo en la pradera:
cómo podía nadie distinguirlo
si era el inseparable, el elemento,
tierra, carbón o mar vestido de hombre?

Donde vivió crecía
cuanto el hombre tocaba:
la piedra hostil,
quebrada
por sus manos,
se convertía en orden
y una a una formaron
la recta claridad del edificio,
hizo el pan con sus manos,
movilizó los trenes,
se poblaron de pueblos las distancias,
otros hombres crecieron,
llegaron las abejas,
y porque el hombre crea y multiplica

so only when the poor man was able
did he come back to life, unnoticed.

He was the man all right, with no inheritance,
no cattle, no coat of arms,
and he did not stand out from others,
others who were himself;
from above he was gray, like clay,
he was drab, like leather,
he was yellow harvesting wheat,
he was black down in the mine,
stone-colored in the castle,
in the fishing boat the color of tuna,
horse-colored on the prairies—
how could anyone distinguish him
if he were inseparable from his element,
earth, coal, or sea in a man's form?

Where he lived, everything
the man touched would grow—
the hostile stones
broken
by his hands
took shape and line
and one by one assumed
the sharp forms of buildings;
he made bread with his hands,
set the trains running;
the distances filled with towns,
other men grew,
the bees arrived,
and through the man's creating and multiplying,

la primavera caminó al mercado
entre panaderías y palomas.

El padre de los panes fue olvidado,
él que cortó y anduvo, machacando
y abriendo surcos, acarreando arena,
cuando todo existió ya no existía,
él daba su existencia, eso era todo.
Salió otra parte a trabajar, y luego
se fue a morir rodando
como piedra del río:
aguas abajo lo llevó la muerte.

Yo, que lo conocí, lo vi bajando
hasta no ser sino lo que dejaba:
calles que apenas pudo conocer,
casas que nunca y nunca habitaría.

Y vuelvo a verlo, y cada día espero.

Lo veo en su ataúd y resurrecto.

Lo distingo entre todos
los que son sus iguales
y me parece que no puede ser,
que así no vamos a ninguna parte,
que suceder así no tiene gloria.

Yo creo que en el trono debe estar
este hombre, bien calzado y coronado.

spring wandered into the marketplace
between bakeries and doves.

The father of the loaves was forgotten,
the one who cut and trudged, beating
and opening paths, shifting sand;
when everything came into being, he no longer existed.
He gave away his existence, that was all.
He went somewhere else to work and ultimately
he went toward death, rolling
like a river stone;
death carried him off downstream.

I who knew him saw him go down
until he existed only in what he was leaving—
streets he could scarcely be aware of,
houses he never never would inhabit.

And I come back to see him, and every day I wait.

I see him in his coffin and resurrected.

I pick him out from all
the others who are his equals
and it seems to me that this cannot be,
that this way leads us nowhere,
that to continue so has no glory.

I believe that heaven must encompass
this man, properly shod and crowned.

Creo que los que hicieron tantas cosas
deben ser dueños de todas las cosas.
Y los que hacen el pan deben comer!

Y deben tener luz los de la mina!

Basta ya de encadenados grises!

Basta de pálidos desaparecidos!

Ni un hombre más que pase sin que reine.

Ni una sola mujer sin su diadema.

Para todas las manos guantes de oro.

Frutas de sol a todos los oscuros!

Yo conocí aquel hombre y cuando pude,
cuando ya tuve ojos en la cara,
cuando ya tuve la voz en la boca
lo busqué entre las tumbas, y le dije
apretándole un brazo que aún no era polvo:

"Todos se irán, tú quedarás viviente.

Tú encendiste la vida.

Tú hiciste lo que es tuyo."

I think that those who made so many things
ought to be owners of everything.
That those who make bread ought to eat.

That those in the mine should have light.

Enough now of gray men in chains!

Enough of the pale lost ones!

Not another man should pass except as a ruler.

Not one woman without her diadem.

Gloves of gold for every hand.

Fruits of the sun for all the shadowy ones!

I knew that man, and when I could,
when I still had eyes in my head,
when I still had a voice in my throat,
I sought him among the tombs and I said to him,
pressing his arm that still was not dust:

"Everything will pass, you will still be living.

You set fire to life.

You made what is yours."

Por eso nadie se moleste cuando
parece que estoy solo y no estoy solo,
no estoy con nadie y hablo para todos:

Alguien me está escuchando y no lo saben,
pero aquellos que canto y que lo saben
siguen naciendo y llenarán el mundo.

So let no one be perturbed when
I seem to be alone and am not alone;
I am not without company and I speak for all.

Someone is hearing me without knowing it,
but those I sing of, those who know,
go on being born and will overflow the world.

ALASTAIR REID

PLENOS PODERES

A puro sol escribo, a plena calle,
a pleno mar, en donde puedo canto,
sólo la noche errante me detiene
pero en su interrupción recojo espacio,
recojo sombra para mucho tiempo.

El trigo negro de la noche crece
mientras mis ojos miden la pradera
y así de sol a sol hago las llaves:
busco en la oscuridad las cerraduras
y voy abriendo al mar las puertas rotas
hasta llenar armarios con espuma.

Y no me canso de ir y de volver,
no me para la muerte con su piedra,
no me canso de ser y de no ser.

A veces me pregunto si de dónde
si de padre o de madre o cordillera
heredé los deberes minerales,

los hilos de un océano encendido
y sé que sigo y sigo porque sigo
y canto porque canto y porque canto.

No tiene explicación lo que acontece
cuando cierro los ojos y circulo
como entre dos canales submarinos,

FULLY EMPOWERED

I write in the clear sun, in the teeming street,
at full sea tide, in a place where I can sing;
only the wayward night inhibits me,
but, interrupted by it, I recover space,
I gather shadows to last a long time.

The black crop of the night is growing
while my eyes in the meantime measure the plain.
So, from sun to sun, I forge the keys.
In the half-light, I look for locks
and keep on opening broken doors to the sea
until I fill the cupboards up with foam.

And I never weary of going and returning.
Death in its stone aspect does not stop me.
I am weary neither of being nor of nonbeing.

Sometimes I wonder where—
from father or mother or the mountains—
I inherited all my mineral obligations,

the threads spreading from a sea on fire;
and I know I go on and go on because I go on
and I sing because I sing and because I sing.

There is no way of explaining what happens
when I close my eyes and waver
as between two underwater channels—

uno a morir me lleva en su ramaje
y el otro canta para que yo cante.

Así pues de no ser estoy compuesto
y como el mar asalta el arrecife
con cápsulas saladas de blancura
y retrata la piedra con la ola,
así lo que en la muerte me rodea
abre en mí la ventana de la vida
y en pleno paroxismo estoy durmiendo.
A plena luz camino por la sombra.

one lifts me in its branches toward dying
and the other sings in order that I may sing.

And so I am formed out of nonbeing,
and as the sea goes battering at a reef
in wave on wave of salty white-tops
and drags back stones in its ebb,
so what there is of death surrounding me
opens in me a window out to living,
and, in a spasm of being, I am asleep.
In the full light of day, I walk in the shade.

ALASTAIR REID

FROM

Memorial de
Isla Negra

Isla Negra

(1962–64)

EL SEXO

La puerta en el crepúsculo,
en verano.
Las últimas carretas
de los indios,
una luz indecisa
y el humo
de la selva quemada
que llega hasta las calles
con los aromas rojos,
la ceniza
del incendio distante.

Yo, enlutado,
severo,
ausente,
con pantalones cortos,
piernas flacas,
rodillas
y ojos que buscan
súbitos tesoros,
Rosita y Josefina
al otro lado
de la calle,
llenas de dientes y ojos,
llenas de luz y con voz como pequeñas
guitarras escondidas
que me llaman.
Y yo crucé
la calle, el desvarío,

SEX

The door at twilight,
in summer.
The last passing carts
of the Indians,
a wavering light
and the smoke
of forest fires
which comes as far as the streets
with the smell of red,
ash
of the distant burning.

I, in mourning,
grave,
withdrawn,
shorts,
thin legs,
knees,
and eyes on the look for
sudden treasures;
Rosita and Josefina
on the other side
of the street,
all teeth and eyes,
full of light, voices
like small, concealed guitars,
calling me.
And I crossed
the street, confused,

temeroso,
y apenas
llegué
me susurraron,
me tomaron las manos,
me taparon los ojos
y corrieron conmigo,
con mi inocencia
a la Panadería.

Silencio de mesones, grave
casa del pan, deshabitada,
y allí las dos
y yo su prisionero
en manos de
la primera Rosita,
la última Josefina.
Quisieron
desvestirme,
me fugué, tembloroso,
y no podía
correr, mis piernas
no podían
llevarme. Entonces
las
fascinadoras
produjeron
ante mi vista
un milagro:
un minúsculo
nido
de avecilla salvaje

terrified;
and hardly
had I arrived
than they whispered to me,
they took my hands,
they covered my eyes
and they ran with me
and my innocence
to the bakehouse.

Silence of great tables, the serious
place of bread, empty of people;
and there, the two of them
and I, prisoner
in the hands of
the first Rosita
and the final Josefina.
They wanted to
undress me.
I fled, trembling,
but I couldn't
run, my legs
couldn't
carry me. Then
the
enchantresses
brought out
before my eyes
a miracle:
the tiny nest
of a small wild bird

con cinco huevecitos,
con cinco uvas blancas,
un pequeño
racimo
de la vida del bosque,
y yo estiré
la mano,
mientras
trajinaban mi ropa,
me tocaban,
examinaban con sus grandes ojos
su primer hombrecito.

Pasos pesados, toses,
mi padre que llegaba
con extraños,
y corrimos
al fondo y a la sombra
las dos piratas
y yo su prisionero,
amontonados
entre las telarañas, apretados
bajo un mesón, temblando,
mientras el milagro,
el nido
de los huevecitos celestes
cayó y luego los pies de los intrusos
demolieron fragancia y estructura.
Pero, con las dos niñas
en la sombra

with five little eggs,
with five white grapes,
a small
cluster
of forest life,
and I reached out
my hand
while
they fumbled with my clothes,
touched me,
studied with their great eyes
their first small man.

Heavy footsteps, coughing,
my father arriving
with strangers,
and we ran
deep into the dark,
the two pirates
and I, their prisoner,
huddled
among spiderwebs,
squeezed
under a great table, trembling,
while the miracle,
the nest
with its small light-blue eggs,
fell and eventually the intruders' feet
crushed its shape and its fragrance.
But, with the two girls
in the dark,

y el miedo,
entre el olor de la harina,
los pasos espectrales,
la tarde que se convertía en sombra,
yo sentí que cambiaba
algo
en mi sangre
y que subía a mi boca,
a mis manos,
una eléctrica
flor,
la
flor
hambrienta
y pura
del deseo.

and fear,
with the smell of flour,
the phantom steps,
the afternoon gradually darkening,
I felt that something was
changing
in my blood
and that to my mouth,
to my hands,
was rising
an electric
flower,
the
hungry,
shining
flower
of desire.

ALASTAIR REID

LA POESÍA

Y fue a esa edad . . . Llegó la poesía
a buscarme. No sé, no sé de dónde
salió, de invierno o río.
No sé cómo ni cuándo,
no, no eran voces, no eran
palabras, ni silencio,
pero desde una calle me llamaba,
desde las ramas de la noche,
de pronto entre los otros,
entre fuegos violentos
o regresando solo,
allí estaba sin rostro
y me tocaba.

Yo no sabía qué decir, mi boca
no sabía
nombrar,
mis ojos eran ciegos,
y algo golpeaba en mi alma,
fiebre o alas perdidas,
y me fui haciendo solo,
descifrando
aquella quemadura,
y escribí la primera línea vaga,
vaga, sin cuerpo, pura
tontería,
pura sabiduría
del que no sabe nada,
y vi de pronto

And it was at that age . . . poetry arrived
in search of me. I don't know, I don't know where
it came from, from winter or a river.
I don't know how or when,
no, they were not voices, they were not
words, not silence,
but from a street it called me,
from the branches of night,
abruptly from the others,
among raging fires
or returning alone,
there it was, without a face,
and it touched me.

I didn't know what to say, my mouth
had no way
with names,
my eyes were blind.
Something knocked in my soul,
fever or forgotten wings,
and I made my own way,
deciphering
that fire,
and I wrote the first, faint line,
faint, without substance, pure
nonsense,
pure wisdom
of someone who knows nothing;
and suddenly I saw

el cielo
desgranado
y abierto,
planetas,
plantaciones palpitantes,
la sombra perforada,
acribillada
por flechas, fuego y flores,
la noche arrolladora, el universo.

Y yo, mínimo ser,
ebrio del gran vacío
constelado,
a semejanza, a imagen
del misterio,
me sentí parte pura
del abismo,
rodé con las estrellas,
mi corazón se desató en el viento.

the heavens
unfastened
and open,
planets,
palpitating plantations,
the darkness perforated,
riddled
with arrows, fire, and flowers,
the overpowering night, the universe.

And I, tiny being,
drunk with the great starry
void,
likeness, image of
mystery,
felt myself a pure part
of the abyss.
I wheeled with the stars.
My heart broke loose with the wind.

ALASTAIR REID

AY! MI CIUDAD PERDIDA

Me gustaba Madrid y ya no puedo
verlo, no más, ya nunca más, amarga
es la desesperada certidumbre
como de haberse muerto uno también al tiempo
que morían los míos, como si se me hubiera
ido a la tumba la mitad del alma,
y allí yaciere entre llanuras secas,
prisiones y presidios,
aquel tiempo anterior cuando aún no tenía
sangre la flor, coágulos la luna.
Me gustaba Madrid por arrabales,
por calles que caían a Castilla
como pequeños ríos de ojos negros:
era el final de un día:
calles de cordeleros y toneles,
trenzas de esparto como cabelleras,
duelas arqueadas desde
donde
algún día
iba a volar el vino a un ronco reino,
calles de los carbones,
de las madererías,
calles de las tabernas anegadas
por el caudal
del duro Valdepeñas
y calles solas, secas, de silencio
compacto como adobe,
e ir y saltar los pies sin alfabeto,
sin guía, ni buscar, ni hallar, viviendo

OH, MY LOST CITY

I liked Madrid and now
I can't see it again, not anymore, a bitter
but desperate certainty, coming
from having died at the time
when my friends died, as if
half of my spirit had gone to the grave
and lay there among dry plains,
prisons and prisoners,
and an earlier time when the towers
were not stained with blood, the moon with blood clots.
I liked Madrid, its outskirts,
its streets that fell away to Castile
like little rivers of black eyes.
It was the ending of a day—
streets of ropeworks and barrels,
tresses of esparto like hair,
bent staves from which
one day
wine
would take flight to its raucous kingdom,
streets of coal,
lumberyards,
streets of taverns overflowing
with an abundance
of the hard wine of Valdepeñas,
and solitary streets, dry,
with a silence as tight as adobe,
and the going and coming of my unlettered feet,
unguided, neither looking nor finding, living

aquello que vivía
callando con aquellos
terrones, ardiendo
con las piedras
y al fin callado el grito de una ventana, el canto
de un pozo, el sello
de una gran carcajada
que rompía
con vidrios
el crepúsculo, y aún
más acá,
en la garganta
de la ciudad tardía,
caballos polvorientos,
carros de ruedas rojas,
y el aroma
de las panaderías al cerrarse
la corola nocturna
mientras enderezaba mi vaga dirección
hacia Cuatro Caminos, al número
3
de la calle Wellingtonia
en donde me esperaba
bajo dos ojos con chispas azules
la sonrisa que nunca he vuelto a ver
en el rostro
—plenilunio rosado—
de Vicente Aleixandre
que dejé allí a vivir con sus ausentes.

what was lived,
being silent with
those plots, burning
with the stones,
and finally silent, the screech of a window, the song
of a well, the sound
of a great guffaw
which broke
the glass
of twilight, and even
closer,
in the throat
of the evening city,
dusty horses,
carts with red wheels,
and the aroma
of closing bakeries,
the crown of night,
as I turned vaguely toward
Cuatro Caminos,
Calle Wellingtonia,
number 3,
where, with eyes like blue sparks,
face like a pink full moon,
a smile I have never gone back to see,
Vicente Aleixandre
was waiting for me.
I left him there to live with his dead friends.

ALASTAIR REID

TAL VEZ CAMBIÉ DESDE ENTONCES

A mi patria llegué con otros ojos
que la guerra me puso
debajo de los míos.
Otros ojos quemados
en la hoguera,
salpicados
por llanto mío y sangre de los otros,
y comencé a mirar y a ver más bajo,
más al fondo inclemente
de las asociaciones. La verdad
que antes no despegaba de su cielo
como una estrella fue,
se convirtió en campana,
oí que me llamaba
y que se congregaban otros hombres
al llamado. De pronto
las banderas de América,
amarillas, azules, plateadas,
con sol, estrella y amaranto y oro
dejaron a mi vista
territorios desnudos,
pobres gentes de campos y caminos,
labriegos asustados, indios muertos,
a caballo, mirando ya sin ojos,
y luego el boquerón infernal de las minas
con el carbón, el cobre y el hombre devastados,
pero eso no era todo
en las repúblicas,
sino algo sin piedad, sin amasijo:

PERHAPS I'VE CHANGED SINCE THEN

I arrived in my country with different eyes
which the war had grafted
underneath my own,
other eyes burned
in the bonfire,
splashed
by my own tears and the blood of the others,
and I began to look and to see deeper,
into the troubled depths
of human connections. The truth
which before did not come loose from the sky
as a star does
changed into a bell.
I realized that it was calling me
and that other men were rallying
to its call. Suddenly
the banners of America,
yellow, blue, silver,
with sun and star and amaranth and gold,
left in my vision
naked territories,
poor people from fields and roads,
frightened farmers, dead Indians,
on horseback, gazing without any eyes,
and then the terrible maw of the mines
with coal, copper, and devastated men,
but that was not all
in the republics:
there was something else, pitiless, unformed.

arriba un galopante, un frío soberbio
con todas sus medallas,
manchado en los martirios
o bien los caballeros en el Club
con vaivén discursivo entre las alas
de la vida dichosa
mientras el pobre ángel oscuro,
el pobre remendado,
de piedra en piedra andaba y anda aún
descalzo y con tan poco qué comer
que nadie sabe cómo sobrevive.

A man on horseback, a cold arrogance,
all his medals
stained by martyred blood,
or else the gentlemen in the club
in their talkative rocking chairs, on the wings
of a good life,
while the poor anonymous angel,
the poor patched-up one,
walked from stone to stone and is still walking
barefoot and with so little to eat
that nobody knows how he survives.

ALASTAIR REID

PARA LA ENVIDIA

De uno a uno saqué los envidiosos
de mi propia camisa, de mi piel,
los vi junto a mí mismo cada día,
los contemplé
en el reino transparente
de una gota de agua:
los amé cuanto pude: en su desdicha
o en la ecuanimidad de sus trabajos:
y hasta ahora no sé
cómo ni cuándo
substituyeron nardo o limonero
por silenciosa arruga
y una grieta anidó donde se abriera
la estrella regular de la sonrisa.

Aquella grita de un hombre en la boca!

Aquella miel que fue substituida!

El grave viento de la edad
volando
trajo polvo, alimentos,
semillas separadas del amor,
pétalos enrollados de serpiente,
ceniza cruel del odio muerto
y todo
fructificó en la herida de la boca,
funcionó la pasión generatriz

I plucked the envious ones, one by one,
from my shirt, from my skin.
I saw them all around me every day.
I brooded on them
in the transparent kingdom
of a drop of water.
I loved them as much as I could, in their misfortune,
or in the equanimity of their labors,
and even now I have no idea
how or when
they replaced lilies and lemon trees
with a silent frown
or, where an ordinary smile should have been,
a gash set in.

That gash of a mouth!

All that honey that was replaced!

The heavy wind of age
brought in its flight
dust, food,
seeds split off from love,
petals wound with snakes,
cruel ash of dead hatred,
and everything
flourished in the wounded mouth.
A web of passions started up

y el triste sedimento del olvido
germinó, levantando la corola,
la medusa violeta de la envidia.

Qué haces tú, Pedro, cuando sacas peces?
Los devuelves al mar, rompes la red,
cierras los ojos ante el incentivo
de la profundidad procreadora?

Ay! Yo confieso mi pecado puro!
Cuanto saqué del mar,
coral, escama,
cola del arcoiris,
pez o palabra o planta plateada
o simplemente piedra submarina,
yo la erigí, le di la luz de mi alma.

Yo, pescador, recogí lo perdido
y no hice daño a nadie en mis trabajos.

No hice daño, o tal vez herí de muerte
al que quiso nacer y recibió
el canto de mi desembocadura
que silenció su condición bravía:
al que no quiso
navegar en mi pecho,
y desató
su propia fuerza,

and the woeful dregs of being forgotten
gave root to the spreading tentacles,
the violet medusa of envy.

When you catch fish, Pedro, what do you do?
Do you throw them back, rip up your net,
close your eyes to the urges
in the vast web of procreation?

I confess to my own sin!
Whatever I took from the sea,
coral, fish scales,
rainbow tail,
fish or word or silvered leaf,
or even an underwater stone,
I raised it up, I gave it the light of my spirit.

Fisherman myself, I gathered whatever was lost,
and my efforts harmed no one.

I did no harm, or maybe I did to death
someone who wanted the light himself, and got instead
me, emptying myself in song,
which silenced his untamed ways,
someone who didn't want
to swim in my breast,
and cut out
on his own,

pero vino el viento
y se llevó su voz y no nacieron
aquellos que querían ver la luz.

Tal vez el hombre crece y no respeta,
como el árbol del bosque, el albedrío
de lo que lo rodea,
y es de pronto
no sólo la raíz, sino la noche,
y no sólo da frutos, sino sombra,
sombra y noche que el tiempo y el follaje
abandonaron en el crecimiento
hasta que desde la humedad yacente
en donde esperan las germinaciones
no se divisan dedos de la luz:
el gratuito sol le fue negado
a la semilla hambrienta
y a plena oscuridad desencadena
el alma un desarrollo atormentado.

Tal vez no sé, no supe, no sabía.

No tuve tiempo en mis preocupaciones
de ver, de oír, de acechar y palpar
lo que estaba pasando, y por amor
pensé que mi deber era cantar,
cantar creciendo y olvidando siempre,
agonizando como resistiendo:

but the wind came
and carried off his voice,
and they were never born,
those who longed to see light.

The tree is part of the forest, but perhaps a man
can grow up ignoring
the bent of everything around him,
and quite suddenly
it's not just roots but darkness,
not just fruit but shadow,
shadow and night which time and foliage
left behind as they grew,
till in the close dampness
where the seeds expected to swell
there is no trace of the fingering light.
The gift of the sun is denied
the hungry seed
and deep in darkness the spirit
unwinds in its own contortions.

Perhaps I don't know, perhaps I didn't know,
perhaps I never knew.

Preoccupied as I was, I had no time
to see, or hear, or seek out, or face
all that was happening, and for love's sake
I believed my obligation was to sing,
to sing as I grew and left my life behind,
out of the pain of the struggle.

era mi amor, mi oficio
en la mañana entre los carpinteros,
bebiendo con los húsares, de noche,
desatar la escritura de mi canto
y yo creí cumplir,
ardiente o separado
del fuego,
cerca del manantial o en la ceniza,
creí que dando cuanto yo tenía,
hiriéndome para no dormir,
a todo sueño, a toda hora, a toda vida,
con mi sangre y con mis meditaciones,
y con lo que aprendí de cada cosa,
del clavel, de su generosidad,
de la madera y su paz olorosa,
del propio amor, del río, de la muerte,
con lo que me otorgó la ciudad y la tierra,
con lo que yo arranqué de una ola verde,
o de una casa que dejó vacía
la guerra, o de una lámpara
que halló encendida en medio del otoño,
así como del hombre y de sus máquinas,
del pequeño empleado y su aflicción,
o del navío navegando en la niebla:
con todo y, más que todo, con lo que yo debía
a cada hombre por su propia vida
hice yo lo posible por pagar, y no tuve
otra moneda que mi propia sangre.

Ahora qué hago con éste y con el otro?

It was my dedication, my function,
alongside carpenters in the morning,
drinking at night with the horsemen,
to pour out my song in writing,
and I thought I was doing it,
on fire or far away
from the fire,
close to the source or out of the ashes;
I thought that by giving all I had,
jabbing myself to keep myself awake,
giving my whole vision, my whole time, my whole life,
my blood and all my thinking,
and what I learned from every thing,
the generosity of carnations,
wood and its sweet-smelling peace,
love itself, rivers, death,
all I was given by the city, by the earth,
all I gathered in from a green wave,
or a house left empty by war,
or a lamp I found lit
in the middle of autumn,
and men too, and their machinery,
working men and their troubles,
or the ship steering through the fog:
all that, more than all, all that I owed
to every man for the life in him,
I did what I could to repay, and I had
no other currency but my own blood.

So what do I do now with this man and the other?

Qué puedo hacer para restituir
lo que yo no robé? Por qué la primavera
me trajo a mí una corona amarilla
y quién anduvo hostil y enmarañado
buscándola en el bosque? Ahora
tal vez es tarde ya para encontrar
y volcar en la copa del rencor
la verdad atrasada y cristalina.

Tal vez el tiempo endureció la voz,
la boca, la piedad del ofendido,
y ya el reloj no podrá volver
a la consagración de la ternura.

El odio despiadado tuvo tiempo
de construir un pabellón furioso
y destinarme una corona cruel
con espinas sangrientas y oxidadas.
Y no fue por orgullo que guardé
el corazón ausente del terror:
ni de mi dolor ensimismado,
ni de las alegrías que sostengo
dispersé
en la venganza
el poderío.

Fue por otra razón, por indefenso.

Fue porque a cada mordedura
el día
que llegaba
me separaba de un nuevo dolor,

What can I do to give back
what I never stole? Why did the spring
bring me a yellow crown
and who, aggrieved and puzzled,
searched for it in the forest?
It's perhaps too late to uncover
the missing clarity of truth
and pour it into his bitter cup.

Maybe time has hardened his voice,
his mouth, his righteousness,
and the clock cannot turn back
to bring us together in tenderness.

Raw hatred took its time
making an outpost of its rage
and prepared for me a savage crown
with rusty, bloodstained spikes.
It wasn't pride that made me keep
my heart at a distance from such terror,
nor did I waste
on revenge
or the pursuit of power
the forces that came from my selfish griefs
or my accumulated joys.

It was something else—my helplessness.

It was because with every taunt
the day
that dawned
detached me from new hurt,

me amarraba las manos y crecía
el liquen en la piedra de mi pecho,
la enredadera se me derramaba,
pequeñas manos verdes me cubrían,
y me fui ya sin puños a los bosques
o me dormí en el título del trébol.

Oh, yo resguardo en mí mismo la avaricia
de mis espadas, lento
en la ira,
gozo
en mi dureza,
pero cuando la tórtola en la torre
trina, y agacha el brazo el alfarero
hacia su barro, haciéndolo vasija,
yo tiemblo y me traspasa
el aire lancinante:
mi corazón se va con la paloma.

Llueve y salgo a probar el aguacero.

Yo salgo a ser lo que amo, la desnuda
existencia del sol en el peñasco,
y lo que crece y crece sin saber
que no puede abolir su crecimiento:
dar grano el trigo: ser innumerable
sin razón: porque así le fue ordenado:
sin orden, sin mandato,
y, entre las rosas que no se reparten,
tal vez esta secreta voluntad,

bound my hands, and lichen
grew on the stone of my breast.
I was overgrown by creeping plants,
small green hands covered me,
and I took to the woods, unfisted,
or slept in care of the clover.

Oh, I am most careful with
my sword's keen edge, I'm slow
to anger,
I rejoice in
my hard nature,
but when the turtledove in the tower
'croons, and the potter stretches his hands
to his clay, raising a bowl,
I tremble, I am pierced through
by the sharp air.
My heart takes off with the dove.

It rains, and I go out to try the shower.

I go out to the being I love, naked presence
of sun on a rock,
everything growing, growing, unaware
that it cannot put an end to its own growing;
the wheat going to grain, multiplying
far beyond reason, so it was ordained,
without order or instruction;
and, among undivided things,
perhaps this secret urge,

esta trepidación de pan y arena,
llegaron a imponer su condición
y no soy yo sino materia viva
que fermenta y levanta sus insignias
en la fecundación de cada día.

Tal vez la envidia, cuando
sacó a brillar contra mí la navaja
y se hizo profesión de algunos cuantos,
agregó a mi substancia un alimento
que yo necesitaba en mis trabajos,
un ácido agresivo que me dio
el estímulo brusco de una hora,
la corrosiva lengua contra el agua.

Tal vez la envidia, estrella
hecha de vidrios rotos
caídos
en una calle amarga,
fue una medalla que condecoró
el pan que doy cantando cada día
y a mi buen corazón de panadero.

this agitation of bread and sand,
imposed its own conditions,
and I'm not me but living matter
fermenting and forming its own shapes
in the fruitfulness of every day.

Perhaps envy, when it flashed
its knife at me
and became the profession of certain people,
gave to my body an extra food
which I needed in my work,
a fierce acid which gave me
sharp stimulation for an odd hour,
corrosive tongue against the water.

Perhaps envy, a star
made from broken glass
fallen
in a bitter street,
was a medal pinned on
the bread I bring, singing, every day,
and my good baker's heart.

ALASTAIR REID

LA MEMORIA

Tengo que acordarme de todos,
recoger las briznas, los hilos
del acontecer harapiento
y metro a metro las moradas,
los largos caminos del tren,
la superficie del dolor.

Si se me extravía un rosal
y confundo noche con liebre
o bien se me desmoronó
todo un muro de la memoria:
tengo que hacer de nuevo el aire,
el vapor, la tierra, las hojas,
el pelo y también los ladrillos,
las espinas que me clavaron,
la velocidad de la fuga.

Tengan piedad para el poeta.

Siempre olvidé con avidez
y en aquellas manos que tuve
sólo cabían inasibles
cosas que no se tocaban,
que se podían comparar
sólo cuando ya no existían.

Era el humo como un aroma,
era el aroma como el humo,
la piel de un cuerpo que dormía

MEMORY

I have to remember everything,
keep track of blades of grass, the threads
of all untidy happenings,
the resting places, inch by inch,
the infinite railroad tracks,
the surfaces of pain.

If I were to misplace one rosebud
and confuse night with a hare,
or even if one whole wall
of my memory were to disintegrate
I am obliged to make over the air,
steam, earth, leaves,
hair, even the bricks,
the thorns which pierced me,
the speed of flight.

Be gentle with the poet.

I was always quick to forget,
and those hands of mine
could only grasp intangibles,
untouchable things
which could only be compared
when they no longer existed.

The smoke was an aroma,
the aroma something like smoke,
the skin of a sleeping body

y que despertó con mis besos,
pero no me pidan la fecha
ni el nombre de lo que soñé,
ni puedo medir el camino
que tal vez no tiene país
o aquella verdad que cambió
que tal vez se apagó de día
y fue luego luz errante
como en la noche una luciérnaga.

which came to life with my kisses;
but don't ask me the date
or the name of what I dreamed—
nor can I measure the road
which may have no country
or that truth that changed
or perhaps turned off by day
to become a wandering light,
a firefly in the dark.

ALASTAIR REID

EL FUTURO ES ESPACIO

El futuro es espacio,
espacio color de tierra,
color de nube,
color de agua, de aire,
espacio negro para muchos sueños,
espacio blanco para toda la nieve,
para toda la música.

Atrás quedó el amor desesperado
que no tenía sitio para un beso,
hay lugar para todos en el bosque,
en la calle, en la casa,
hay sitio subterráneo y submarino,
qué placer es hallar por fin,
                         subiendo
un planeta vacío,
grandes estrellas claras como el vodka
tan transparentes y deshabitadas,
y allí llegar con el primer teléfono
para que hablen más tarde tantos hombres
de sus enfermedades.

Lo importante es apenas divisarse,
gritar desde una dura cordillera
y ver en la otra punta
los pies de una mujer recién llegada.

Adelante, salgamos
del río sofocante

THE FUTURE IS SPACE

The future is space,
earth-colored space,
cloud-colored,
color of water, air,
black space with room for many dreams,
white space with room for all snow,
for all music.

Behind lies despairing love
with no room for a kiss.
There's a place for everyone in forests,
in streets, in houses;
there's an underground space, a submarine space,
but what joy to find in the end,
                              rising,
an empty planet,
great stars clear as vodka,
so uninhabited and so transparent,
and arrive there with the first telephone
so that so many men can later discuss
all their infirmities.

The important thing is to be scarcely aware of oneself,
to scream from a rough mountain range
and see on another peak
the feet of a woman newly arrived.

Come on, let's leave
this suffocating river

en que con otros peces navegamos
desde el alba a la noche migratoria
y ahora en este espacio descubierto
volemos a la pura soledad.

in which we swim with other fish
from dawn to shifting night
and now in this discovered space
let's fly to a pure solitude.

ALASTAIR REID

FROM

Arte de
pájaros

Art of
Birds

(1962–65)

MIGRACIÓN

Todo el día una línea y otra línea,
un escuadrón de plumas,
un navío
palpitaba en el aire,
atravesaba
el pequeño infinito
de la ventana desde donde busco,
interrogo, trabajo, acecho, aguardo.

La torre de la arena
y el espacio marino
se unen allí, resuelven
el canto, el movimiento.

Encima se abre el cielo.

Entonces así fue: rectas, agudas,
palpitantes, pasaron
hacia dónde? Hacia el norte, hacia el oeste,
hacia la claridad,
hacia la estrella,
hacia el peñón de soledad y sal
donde el mar desbarata sus relojes.

Era un ángulo de aves
dirigidas
aquella latitud de hierro y nieve
que avanzaba
sin tregua

MIGRATION

All day, column after column,
a squadron of feathers,
a fluttering airborne
ship
crossed
the tiny infinity
of the window where I search,
question, work, observe, wait.

The tower of sand
and marine space
join there, comprise
song, movement.

Above, the sky unfolds.

So it was: palpitating,
sharp right angles passed
heading northward, westward,
toward open space,
toward the star,
toward the spire of salt and solitude
where the sea casts its clocks to the winds.

It was an angle of birds
steering for
that latitude of iron and snow,
inexorably advancing along

en su camino rectilíneo:
era la devorante rectitud
de una flecha evidente,
los números del cielo que viajaban
a procrear formados
por imperioso amor y geometría.

Yo me empeñé en mirar hasta perder
los ojos y no he visto
sino el orden del vuelo,
la multitud del ala contra el viento:
vi la serenidad multiplicada
por aquel hemisferio transparente
cruzado por la oscura decisión
de aquellas aves en el firmamento.

No vi sino el camino.

Todo siguió celeste.

Pero en la muchedumbre de las aves
rectas a su destino
una bandada y otra dibujaban
victorias
triangulares
unidas por la voz de un solo vuelo,
por la unidad del fuego,
por la sangre,
por la sed, por el hambre,
por el frío,
por el precario día que lloraba
antes de ser tragado por la noche,

their rectilinear road:
the skyborne numbers
flew with the hungry rectitude
of a well-aimed arrow, winging
their way to procreate, formed
by urgent love and geometry.

I kept looking as far as
the eye could see and saw
nothing but orderly flight,
the multitude of wings against the wind:
I saw serenity multiplied
in that transparent hemisphere
crossed by the obscure decision
of those birds in the firmament.

I saw only the flyway.

All remained celestial.

But among the throngs of birds
homing for their destination
flock after flock sketched out
triangular
victories
united by the voice of a single flight,
by the unity of fire,
by blood,
by thirst, by hunger,
by the cold,
by the precarious day that wept
before being swallowed by night,

por la erótica urgencia de la vida:
la unidad de los pájaros
volaba
hacia las desdentadas costas negras,
peñascos muertos, islas amarillas,
donde el sol dura más que su jornada

y en el cálido mar se desarrolla
el pabellón plural de las sardinas.

En la piedra asaltada
por los pájaros
se adelantó el secreto:
piedra, humedad, estiércol, soledad,
fermentarán y bajo el sol sangriento
nacerán arenosas criaturas
que alguna vez regresarán volando
hacia la huracanada luz del frío,
hacia los pies antárticos de Chile.

Ahora cruzan, pueblan la distancia
moviendo apenas en la luz las alas
como si en un latido las unieran,

vuelan sin desprenderse

del cuerpo

migratorio

que en tierra se divide
y se dispersa.

by the erotic urgency of life:
the unity of birds
flew
toward the toothless black coasts,
lifeless pinnacles, yellow isles,
where the sun works overtime

and the plural pavilion of sardines
spreads over the warm sea.

On the stone assaulted
by the birds
the secret was set forth:
stone, moisture, excrement, and solitude
will ferment and beneath the blood-red sun
sandy offspring will be born
and they, too, will one day fly back
to the tempestuous cold light,
to the antarctic feet of Chile.

Now they pass, filling the distance,
a faint flapping of wings against the light,
a throbbing winged unity

that flies without breaking

from the migratory

body

which ashore divides,
disperses.

Sobre el agua, en el aire,
el ave innumerable va volando,
la embarcación es una,
la nave transparente
construye la unidad con tantas alas,
con tantos ojos hacia el mar abiertos
que es una sola paz la que atraviesa
y sólo un ala inmensa se desplaza.

Ave del mar, espuma migratoria,
ala del sur, del norte, ala de ola,
racimo desplegado por el vuelo,
multiplicado corazón hambriento,
llegarás, ave grande, a desgranar
el collar de los huevos delicados
que empolla el viento y nutren las arenas
hasta que un nuevo vuelo multiplica
otra vez vida, muerte, desarrollo,
gritos mojados, caluroso estiércol,
y otra vez a nacer, a partir, lejos
del páramo y hacia otro páramo.

Lejos
de aquel silencio, huid, aves del frío,
hacia un vasto silencio rocalloso
y desde el nido hasta el errante número,
flechas del mar, dejadme
la húmeda gloria del transcurso,
la permanencia insigne de las plumas
que nacen, mueren, duran y palpitan

Above the water, in the sky,
the innumerable bird flies on,
the vessel is one,
the transparent ship
builds unity with so many wings,
with so many eyes opened to the sea,
sails over a singular peacefulness
with the movement of one immense wing.

Seabird, migratory foam,
wing from north and south, wave wing,
cluster deployed by flight,
multiplied hungry heart,
you will arrive, great bird, to strip
from the necklace the fragile eggs to be
hatched by the wind and nourished by the sand
until another flight again
multiplies life, death, growth,
wet cries, hot dung,
being born again, and leaving, far
from the windy waste to another windy waste.

Far
from that silence, flee, polar birds,
to the vast rocky silence
and from the nest to the errant number,
sea arrows, bequeath me
the wet glory of time elapsed,
the renowned permanence of feathers
that are born, that die, endure, and throb,

creando pez a pez su larga espada,
crueldad contra crueldad la propia luz
y a contraviento y contramar, la vida.

creating fish by fish their long sword,
cruelty against cruelty, the very light
and against the wind and the sea, life.

JACK SCHMITT

FROM

Las manos
del día

The Hands
of Day

(1967–68)

EN VIETNAM

Y quién hizo la guerra?

Desde anteayer está sonando.

Tengo miedo.

Suena como una piedra
contra el muro,
como un trueno con sangre,
como un monte muriendo:
es el mundo
que yo no hice.
Que tú no hiciste.
Que hicieron.
Quién lo amenaza con dedos terribles?
Quién quiere degollarlo?
Verdad que parecía estar naciendo?
Y quién lo mata ahora porque nace?

Tiene miedo el ciclista,
el arquitecto.
Se esconde la mamá con su niño y sus senos,
en el barro.
Duerme en la cueva esta mamá y de pronto
la guerra,
viene grande la guerra,
viene llena de fuego
y ya quedaron muertos,

IN VIETNAM

And who made war?

It's been pounding since the day before yesterday.

I'm afraid.

It pounds like a stone
against the wall,
like thunder with blood,
like a dying mountain.
This is a world
I didn't make.
You didn't make it.
They made it.
Who threatens it with terrible fingers?
Who wants it decapitated?
Wasn't it about to come into being?
And who kills it now it is born?

The cyclist is afraid,
so is the architect.
The mother with a child and her breasts
hides in the mud.
This mother sleeps in the cave and suddenly,
war,
war arrives big,
arrives full of fire
and already dead,

muertos
la madre con su leche y con su hijo.

Murieron en el barro.

Oh dolor, desde entonces
hasta ahora
hay que estar con el barro
hasta las sienes
cantando y disparando? Santo Dios!
Si te lo hubieran dicho
antes de ser, antes de casi ser,
si por lo menos
te hubieran susurrado
que tus parientes o tus no parientes,
hijos de aquella risa del amor,
hijos de esperma humana,
y de aquella fragancia
a nuevo lunes y a camisa fresca
tenían que morir tan repentinamente
y sin saber jamás de qué se trata!

Son los mismos
que vienen a matarnos,
sí, son los mismos
que vendrán a quemarnos,
sí, los mismos,
los gananciosos y los jactanciosos,
los sonrientes que jugaban tanto
y que ganaban tanto,
ahora
por el aire

dead
are the mother with her milk and her son.

They died in the mud.

Oh pain! From then
till now,
should one stay covered with mud
up to the temples,
singing and shooting? Holy God!
If only you had been told
before you lived, almost before you lived . . .
If at least
they had whispered it
to your relatives and nonrelatives,
children of love's laughter,
children of human sperm,
of that fragrance
in a new Monday and with a fresh shirt . . .
But they had to die so suddenly,
without ever knowing what it was all about!

They are the same ones
who come to kill us,
yes, the same ones
who come to burn us,
yes, the same ones,
the winners and the braggers,
the smiling ones who enjoyed so much
and took so much,
now
by air

vienen, vendrán, vinieron,
a matarnos el mundo.

Han dejado una charca
de padre, madre e hijo:
busquemos
en ella,
busca tus propios huesos y tu sangre,
búscalos en el barro de Vietnam,
búscalos entre otros tantos huesos:
ahora quemados ya no son de nadie,
son de todos,
son nuestros huesos, busca
tu muerte en esa muerte,
porque están acechándote los mismos
y te destinan a ese mismo barro.

they come, will come, they came,
to kill the world within us.

They have left a pool
made of father, mother, and child.
Let us look
in it,
look for our own blood and bones,
look for them in the mud of Vietnam,
look for them among so many other bones;
they're charred, they no longer belong to anyone
but to everyone,
our bones are burnt,
look for your death in that death,
because they are after you too,
and the fate they bring you is that selfsame mud.

ILAN STAVANS

VERBO

Voy a arrugar esta palabra,
voy a torcerla,
sí,
es demasiado lisa,
es como si un gran perro o un gran río
le hubiera repasado lengua o agua
durante muchos años.

Quiero que en la palabra
se vea la aspereza,
la sal ferruginosa,
la fuerza desdentada
de la tierra,
la sangre
de los que hablaron y de los que no hablaron.

Quiero ver la sed
adentro de las sílabas:
quiero tocar el fuego
en el sonido:
quiero sentir la oscuridad
del grito. Quiero
palabras ásperas
como piedras vírgenes.

VERB

I'm going to wrinkle this word,
twist it,
yes,
it's too smooth,
as if the tongue
of a big dog or a big river's water
had washed it
for years and years.

I want to see
roughness in the word,
ironlike salt,
earth's
toothless strength,
the blood
of those who spoke out and those who didn't.

I want to see thirst
deep in its syllables.
I want to touch fire
in the sound.
I want to feel
the darkness of a scream.
I want rough words
like virginal stones.

ILAN STAVANS

333

FROM

Fin del mundo

World's End

(1968–69)

TRISTÍSIMO SIGLO

El siglo de los desterrados,
el libro de los desterrados,
el siglo pardo, el libro negro,
esto es lo que debo dejar
escrito y abierto en el libro,
desenterrándolo del siglo
y desangrándolo en el libro.

Porque yo viví el matorral
de los perdidos en la selva:
en la selva de los castigos.
Yo conté las manos cortadas
y las montañas de cenizas
y los sollozos separados
y los anteojos sin ojos
y los cabellos sin cabeza.

Luego busqué por el mundo
a quienes perdieron la patria
llevando donde las llevé
sus banderitas derrotadas
o sus estrellas de Jacob
o sus pobres fotografías.

Yo también conocí el destierro.

Pero, nacido caminante
volví con las manos vacías
a este mar que me reconoce,

THE SADDEST CENTURY

The century of émigrés,
the book of homelessness —
gray century, black book.
This is what I ought to leave
written in the open book,
digging it out from the century,
tinting the pages with spilled blood.

I lived the abundance
of those lost in the jungle:
in the jungle of punishment.
I counted the cutoff hands
and the mountains of ash
and the fragmented cries
and the without-eyes glasses
and the headless hair.

Then I searched the world
for those who lost their country,
pointlessly carrying
their defeated little flags,
their Stars of David,
their miserable photographs.

I too knew homelessness.

But as a seasoned wanderer,
I returned empty-handed
to this sea that knows me well.

pero son otros los aún,
los todavía cercenados,
los que siguen dejando atrás
sus amores y sus errores
pensando que tal vez tal vez
y sabiendo que nunca nunca
y así me tocó sollozar
este sollozo polvoriento
de los que perdieron la tierra
y celebrar con mis hermanos
(los que se quedaron allí)
las construcciones victoriosas,
las cosechas de panes nuevos.

But others remain
and are still at bay,
leaving behind their loved ones, their errors,
thinking maybe
but knowing never again
and this is how I ended up sobbing
the dusty sob
intoned by the homeless.
This is the way I ended celebrating
with my brothers (those who remain)
the victorious building,
the harvest of new bread.

ILAN STAVANS

FROM

Jardín de invierno

Winter Garden

(1971–73)

GAUTAMA CRISTO

Los nombres de Dios y en particular de su representante
llamado Jesús o Cristo, según textos y bocas,
han sido usados, gastados y dejados
a la orilla del río de las vidas
como las conchas vacías de un molusco.

Sin embargo, al tocar estos nombres sagrados
y desangrados, pétalos heridos,
saldos de los océanos del amor y del miedo,
algo aún permanece: un labio de ágata,
una huella irisada que aún tiembla en la luz.

Mientras se usaban los nombres de Dios
por los mejores y por los peores, por los limpios y por los sucios
por los blancos y los negros, por ensangrentados asesinos
y por las víctimas doradas que ardieron en napalm,
mientras Nixon con las manos
de Caín bendecía a sus condenados a muerte,
mientras menos y menores huellas divinas se hallaron en la playa,
los hombres comenzaron a estudiar los colores,
el porvenir de la miel, el signo del uranio,
buscaron con desconfianza y esperanza las posibilidades
de matarse y de no matarse, de organizarse en hileras,
de ir más allá, de ilimitarse sin reposo.

Los que cruzamos estas edades con gusto a sangre,
a humo de escombros, a ceniza muerta,
y no fuimos capaces de perder la mirada,
a menudo nos detuvimos en los nombres de Dios,

GAUTAMA CHRIST

The names of God and especially of his representative
called Jesus or Christ, according to texts and mouths,
have been used up, worn down, and deposited
on the riverbank of our lives
like empty mollusk shells.

Nevertheless, touching these sacred names
drained of their blood, wounded petals,
balances of the oceans of love and of fear,
we know something endures there: an agate lip,
an iridescent footprint still shimmering in the light.

While the names of God were spoken
by the best and the worst, by the clean and the dirty,
by whites and blacks, by bloodstained assassins
and golden brown victims who blazed with napalm,
while Nixon with the hands
of Cain blessed those he had condemned to death,
when fewer and smaller divine footprints were found on the beach,
men began to examine the colors,
the promise of honey, the symbol for uranium,
with suspicion and hope they studied the possibilities
of killing and not killing each other, of organizing themselves in rows,
of going even further, of making themselves limitless, without rest.

We who live through these ages with their bloody flavor,
the smell of smoking rubble, of dead ash,
we who were not able to forget the sight
have often stopped to think in the names of God,

los levantamos con ternura porque nos recordaban
a los antecesores, a los primeros, a los que interrogaron,
a los que encontraron el himno que los unió en la desdicha
y ahora viendo los fragmentos vacíos donde habitó aquel hombre
sentimos estas suaves sustancias
gastadas, malgastadas por la bondad y por la maldad.

have raised them up tenderly, because they reminded us
of our ancestors, of the first humans, of those who asked questions,
of those who found the hymn that united them in misery
and now seeing the empty fragments where that man lived
we finger those smooth substances
spent, squandered by good and evil.

WILLIAM O'DALY

FROM

Defectos escogidos

Selected Failings

(1971–73)

EL GRAN ORINADOR

El gran orinador era amarillo
y el chorro que cayó
era una lluvia color de bronce
sobre las cúpulas de las iglesias,
sobre los techos de los automóviles,
sobre las fábricas y los cementerios,
sobre la multitud y sus jardines.

Quién era, dónde estaba?

Era una densidad, líquido espeso
lo que caía
como desde un caballo
y asustados transeúntes
sin paraguas
buscaban hacia el cielo,
mientras las avenidas se anegaban
y por debajo de las puertas
entraban los orines incansables
que iban llenando acequias, corrompiendo
pisos de mármol, alfombras,
escaleras.

Nada se divisaba. Dónde
estaba el peligro?

Qué iba a pasar en el mundo?

THE GREAT URINATOR

The great urinator was yellow
and the stream that came down
was bronze-colored rain
on the domes of churches,
on the roofs of cars,
on factories and cemeteries,
on the populace and their gardens.

Who was it, where was it?

It was a density, thick liquid
falling as from
a horse,
and frightened passersby
with no umbrellas
looked up skyward,
meanwhile avenues were flooding
and urine inexhaustibly flowing
underneath doors,
backing up drains, disintegrating
marble floors, carpets,
staircases.

Nothing could be detected. Where
was this peril?

What was going to happen to the world?

El gran orinador desde su altura
callaba y orinaba.

Qué quiere decir esto?

Soy un simple poeta,
no tengo empeño en descifrar enigmas,
ni en proponer paraguas especiales.

Hasta luego! Saludo y me retiro
a un país donde no me hagan preguntas.

From on high the great urinator
was silent and urinated.

What does this signify?

I am a pale and artless poet
not here to work out riddles
or recommend special umbrellas.

Hasta la vista! I greet you and go off
to a country where they won't ask me questions.

JOHN FELSTINER

Acknowledgments

Grateful acknowledgment is made for permission to reprint the following material:

"I Like for You to Be Still" and "Tonight I Can Write" from *Twenty Love Poems and a Song of Despair*, translated by W. S. Merwin. Copyright © 1969 by W. S. Merwin. Used by permission of Viking Penguin, a division of Penguin Group (USA) Inc.

"Ars Poetica," "Ode to Federico García Lorca," and "Song for the Mothers of Slain Militiamen," from *Residence on Earth*, translated by Donald D. Walsh. Copyright © 1973 by Pablo Neruda and Donald D. Walsh. Reprinted by permission of New Directions Publishing Corp.

"Walking Around," from *Residence on Earth*, translated by Robert Bly. First published in *Neruda and Vallejo: Selected Poems*, edited by Robert Bly. Copyright © 1971 by Robert Bly. Used by permission of the translator.

"I Explain a Few Things," from *Third Residence*, translated by Galway Kinnell. Copyright © 2003 by Galway Kinnell. First published in *The Poetry of Pablo Neruda* (Farrar, Straus and Giroux, 2003). Used by permission of the translator.

"United Fruit Co." and "America, I Do Not Invoke Your Name in Vain," from *Canto General*, translated by Jack Schmitt. Copyright © 1991 by Fundación Pablo Neruda and the Regents of the University of California Press. Used by permission of the publisher.

"I Wish the Woodcutter Would Wake Up I" and "The Strike," from *Canto General*, translated by Robert Bly. First published in *Neruda and Vallejo: Selected Poems*, edited by Robert Bly. Copyright © 1971, 1993 by Robert Bly. Used by permission of the translator.

"Your Hands" and "Your Laughter," from *The Captain's Verses*, translated by Ilan Stavans. Copyright © 2007 by Ilan Stavans. Used by permission of the translator.

"Ode to the Artichoke," "Ode to the Atom," and "Ode to Criticism," from *Elemental Odes*, translated by Margaret Sayers Peden. First published in

The originals in Spanish by Pablo Neruda are published by permission of Carmen Balcells Literary Agency, Barcelona, Spain, and Fundación Pablo Neruda, Santiago, Chile. Versions of the preface appeared, in somewhat different form, in *The Chronicle of Higher Education* and *Review: Latin American Literature and Arts*, published by the Americas Society, New York.

The editor is thankful to Jonathan Galassi for his encouragement and support and to Martín Espada for his editorial suggestions. Several new translations were commissioned for a special issue of *Ploughshares* that he edited. *Gracias*, too, to the following colleagues for their advice: Robert Bly, Rafael Campo, John Felstiner, Edward Hirsch, Galway Kinnell, Philip Levine, Paul Muldoon, Margaret Sayers Peden, Richard Schaaf, Gary Soto, Mark Strand, and Helen Vendler.

Index of First Lines

357